From Four Royal Persian Stars

To

Jesus and the Sun

From Four Royal Persian Stars

To

Jesus and the Sun

By

Eric Norland

iUniverse LLC
Bloomington

FROM FOUR ROYAL PERSIAN STARS TO JESUS AND THE SUN

iUniverse books may be ordered through booksellers or by contacting:

iUniverse LLC
1663 Liberty Drive
Bloomington, IN 47403
www.iuniverse.com
1-800-Authors (1-800-288-4677)

ISBN: 978-1-4917-0816-3 (sc)
ISBN: 978-1-4917-0817-0 (e)

Library of Congress Control Number: 2013917050

Printed in the United States of America.

iUniverse rev. date: 10/17/2013

Table of Contents

Chapter 1

An Introduction to the Four Royal Persian Stars

Fig. 1-1. The four cardinal positions.

Long ago, humans noticed that, when the sun was situated in front of a certain star in a certain constellation along the zodiac, it would be one of the four seasons. This was a very reliable calendar to tell what time of year it was and when to get ready to plant or partake of activities. People remembered this and passed along the information to following generations. But it was very complex information and not well understood. It did not take long for it to be reinterpreted as something of a religious significance and become protected and sacred.

The most ancient historical record of the four royal Persian stars is hinted at in the *Zend Avesta*, or the Persian books of Zarathustra of Zorasterism. Anquetil Duperon, a French Orientalist, translated and published them in 1717. The oldest copy of the *Zend Avesta* is dated to around AD 600, though they appear to have been much older and are derived from an oral tradition from the time of Zarathustra, around 500 BC. Darius the Great most likely worshipped them. One of the verses, Sirozah 13, calls these stars "bright, glorious, they were sacrificed to and worshipped."[1]

A sacred and very ancient text by the Parsees of Pahlavi, the *Bundahishn*, mentions the four stars, "It is Tishtar the chieftain of the east, Sataves the chieftan of the west, Vanand the chieftan of the south, and Haptokring the chieftain of the north."[2]

A French astronomer, Jean Sylvain Bailly, said in his 1789 book, *The History of Ancient Astronomy*, "Tashter who guards the east, Satevis who guards the west, Vanant who

---

[1] *Zend Avesta*, 17.

[2] *Bundahishn*, chapter 2, verse 7.

guards the south and Haftorang the north."[3] He was an accurate astronomer, but after getting caught up in the French Revolution, he was sent to the guillotine in 1793.

French writer Charles Francois Dupuis said in his 1794 book, *Origine de Tous les Cultes*, "These stars (Aldeberan, Regulus, Antares and Fomalhaut) received the pompous denomination of royal stars."[4] This is the first mention of the term "royal star." He also added that Ormusd (God) placed them at the four corners of the sky.[5]

The astronomer George A. Davis Jr. wrote a critical article about the royal Persian stars in *Popular Astronomy* in April 1945. In the article, he incorrectly quotes from the *Bundahishn* that Sataves is south and Vanand is west.[6] He writes that Tishtar is Sirius and associated with the helical rising of a "little cloud." He also admits Tishtar means "cloud." Because there is no "little cloud" near Sirius, this could only be the Pleiades, and it is in Taurus, home of the Pleiades, so Tishtar could be Aldeberan in Taurus. Davis mentions that Sataves is known for water and it would be Aquarius.[7] He said Vanand is a "stinger" like the scorpion.[8]

These, however, seem incorrect and need to be switched around. They are in error, just like he wrongly quoted the *Bundahaisn*. Finally, he says Haptokring is known to have seven stars, so it would be the Big Dipper. However, Leo also has seven stars. Haptokring, therefore, could very well be Leo, and Davis' errors would complete the description of the four royal Persian stars.

So how did they measure the sky long ago? They had very simple but accurate tools that were made to measure where the sun was located and in what zodiacal constellation it was in.

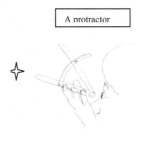

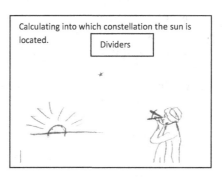

Fig. 1-2. Protractor. Fig. 1-3. Dividers. Fig. 1-4. Astrolabe.

---

[3] Jean Sylvain Bailly, *The History of Ancient Astronomy*, Paris, 1775, p.13, 130, 480, 481.

[4] Charles Francois Dupuis, *Origine de Tous les Cultes*, Paris, 1794, 257–259.

[5] Ibid., 529–530.

[6] George A. Davis, The So Called Royal Stars of Persia, *Popular Astronomy Magazine, U.S.A.*, April 1945, 152.

Adsabs.harvard.edu/full/1945PA.....53..149D

[7] Ibid., 155.

[8] Ibid., 156.

A simple divider and protractor can be used to measure between the stars and the sun. The ancient Greeks used an astrolabe to measure the height of a star above the horizon.[9]

What follows is the correct March 21, 3000 BC, layout of the four royal Persian stars according to Bailly and the *Bundahishn*.

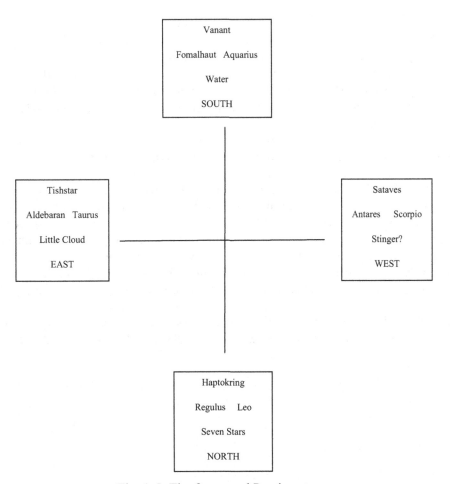

Fig. 1-5. The four royal Persian stars.

The four royal Persian stars are mentioned four times in *Burnham's Celestial Handbook*.[10]

---

[9] *American Peoples Encyclopedia.*

[10] Robert Burnham Jr., *Burnham's Celestial Handbook*, 1057, 1486, 1658, 1807.

Cosmology: A branch of philosophy dealing with the origin processes and structure of the universe.

Fig. 1-6. Cosmology.

What is cosmology? Everyone has a cosmology. No matter how much nor how little a person knows about the world around him or her and the universe, he or she still has a cosmological perspective of his or her place with the universe. In some ways, even creatures find their place where they fit in with the world around them, but this is a very crude way of understanding cosmology.

In this age of rapid Internet knowledge, there is an ever-expanding amount of information regarding our place in the universe. As one learns more and more, one discovers that Earth is a planet with a moon orbiting it and both are in orbit around the sun. One learns of other planets in the solar system and their positions as they orbit the sun. Many stars are nearby, every star we see is a member of our Milky Way galaxy, and other galaxies are around the Milky Way. The universe has about 125 billion other galaxies and appears to have started about 13.7 billion years ago. All of this astronomical information helps a person gain an insight, a greater expanse of knowledge about the universe around him or her, and this adds to his or her cosmology. Cosmology is a very important subject and a big part of one's outlook on the world around him or her because it ultimately informs one of his or her place upon the planet and the way one understands and relates to it and others. It is also very important for the citizens of our world to have a correct cosmological perspective. It gives one a true and understandable view of our predicament and our home planet and the way we fit in with it.

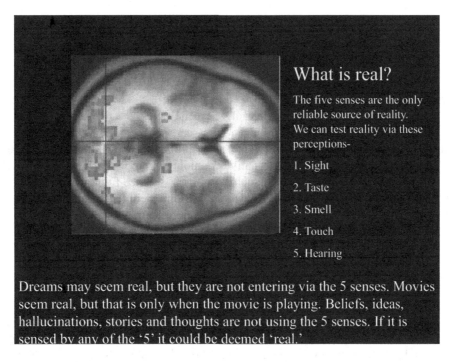

Fig. 1-7. Thoughts on reality.

We all have a common perspective on what is real and can narrow it down to these five senses: sight, taste, smell, touch, and hearing. These basic senses can help us determine whether something is real.

Is carbon monoxide real? It is. One can't smell it. It just requires additional technology to sense it. Is a black hole real? It is. Scientific models and evidence can confirm it.

Another form of testing reality, verifiable facts, should be added. We can use information to explain and prove that something is real. This is verifiable information. One can verify with mathematics or scientific experiments and arrive at a predictable conclusion, which can be falsified or tested to determine if it is real.

The problem with defining what is real is something that happens deep within our brains. Dreams, phobias, mentally distraught emotions, deceased loved ones, and imaginary ideas seem so real in our minds that it is difficult to ascertain reality. Reading a good book or watching a movie may seem real. These fall under an area called delusion, which any of the five senses often cannot prove. While they may seem real, dreams are an idea, which any outside testable information cannot confirm. A thought in the inner brain is not directly connected to the five senses and can be deemed delusional. Just because someone told you something, it does not mean it is true. Use the five senses as a test.

> The popularity of alternative cosmologies is on the rise in the United States.

Fig. 1-8. Alternative cosmologies.
Many people do not understand nor do they care to learn about the scientific explanation for the formation of the universe, sun, and Earth. They either did not learn this information or have been taught an alternative cosmological model. They may have heard their cosmological explanation from sources such as religion, science fiction, entertainment, or other stories handed down. This is alternative cosmology. Some people do not accept science. They accept what they have been told, and they do not want to learn anything else.

> The number-one alternative cosmology is religion.

Fig. 1-9. Religion as cosmology?
Religion indirectly teaches a person a cosmological model of the universe, which is generally not based on scientific facts. It oftentimes comes from myths, stories, conquests, folklores, and mistaken insights into nature. This book hopes to inform you of the astronomy-related misunderstandings people had long ago and the way they turned them into religion.

People spend great amounts of money to support religious activities. This can be observed by the many religions one sees around the world and the many churches one sees in the Yellow Pages. Financial patrons support every congregation. Now, how many science shops do you see in the Yellow Pages? How many telescope shops or scientific suppliers are there? How many do you see on a street corner compared to churches? They do not have the financial reach that religion does to touch everyday people. On a worldwide scale, more money is pumped into religion than just about any other business. They have more financial power to advertise, to promote, to reach out, and to offer free meals than most scientific endeavors do. This, in turn, is where the followers of religion will gain their cosmological model from.

> The popularity of alternative cosmologies is on the rise in the United States.

Fig. 1-10. Alternative cosmologies
So why do so many people give so much financial support to religious organizations when they cannot verify the majority of their claims? The number-one reason is for good luck. People believe that, by supporting a supreme being, they will be given good fortune in turn. Yet most statistics can tell us that religious people are experiencing the same troubles as atheists. They still have bankruptcy, unlawfulness, accidents, health troubles, divorce, and death, no matter what religious foundation they follow.[11]

---

[11] Todd K. Shakelford, *The Oxford Handbook of Evolutionary Perspectives on Violence, Homicide and War*, 447.

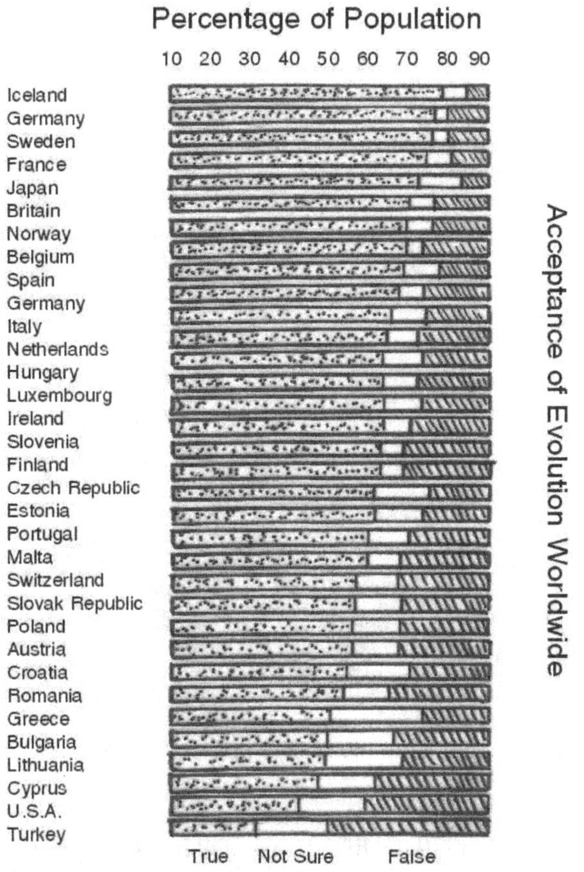

Percentage of Population

Fig. 1-11. Acceptance of evolution

The United States has recently been rated number thirty-three in the world in the acceptance of evolution. [12] This means accepting the science of evolution as a means of explaining the origin of species is rated lower than creationism, the belief that God made everything, in the United States. In some other countries outside of the United States, there is a far greater acceptance of the scientific explanation of evolution over creationism. The United States is currently scaled below countries like Latvia, Belgium, and Croatia in accepting evolution. [13]

[12]

Science, 11 August 2006, Vol.313.   also   old.richarddawkins.net/articles/706-public-acceptance-of-evolution

Fig. 1-12. Using the archaeological method.

The objects at the right side of the above image start from the bottom and work up, beginning with the earliest Syrian village life (1), painted handmade pottery(2), earliest general use of metal(3), cylinder seals from Ur(4), articles from northern Mesopotamia(5), clay figurines(6), painted bowls related to Egyptian pottery(7), cultural relation with the East(8), important pottery, ceramic traces of the "Peoples of the Sea" Syrian Hittite kingdom(9), occupation of the Persian Empire period(10), and the time of St. Paul and early Christian era(11). They are typical of the different periods from 4500 BC to AD 600 and represent the ancient cultural layers found on the slope of Tell Judaidah.

Much the same as an archaeologist can unearth ancient fossils and artifacts, so too can the archaeoastronomer find hidden clues from the past. The most recent information will be nearest to the top, as the more recent civilizations will have left recent items on the highest layer. One has to research farther back in history to find things from long ago. Using very similar techniques accomplishes the historical research in this book.

> If it doesn't have a natural explanation, then there is something suspicious about it.

Fig. 1-13.

We should always question everything and anything and seek to find the natural explanation behind it. Because we are creatures of this planet, made from the biomass that makes up the world we live upon, everything on the planet probably has a natural reason for why it is.

> If we fail to understand nature, then we are doomed to make a crucial mistake.

Fig. 1-14.

One of the dangers in misdiagnosing any problem is the consequences. Nature follows its set of rules. If they are not obeyed, then there is the potential of a negative outcome. By understanding the natural universe, it is more likely that humans can readily adapt and resolve the problem with less of a chance of failure.

Chapter 2

Hypothesis

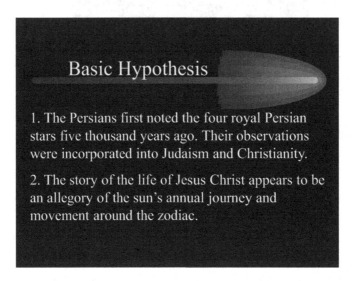

Fig. 2-1.

About five thousand years ago, the Persians noticed four stars were located at specific locations along the ecliptic at which the sun would pass in front of during the four seasons. These four stars and their constellations became integrated into the lore and mythology of religion.

What is even more intriguing is how the four royal Persian stars became integrated with the story of Jesus Christ, the Holy Roman Catholic Church, and St. Peter's Basilica. Finally, I will present modern astronomy to help the reader understand more about where they truly do fit in.

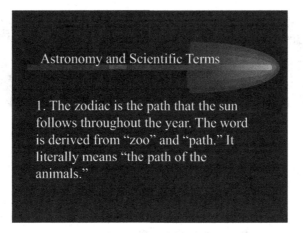

Astronomy and Scientific Terms

1. The zodiac is the path that the sun follows throughout the year. The word is derived from "zoo" and "path." It literally means "the path of the animals."

Fig. 2-2.

The zodiac was very intriguing to the ancients. At its most basic, it is the twelve constellations of which the sun travels through during its yearly journey. The ancients named the route "zodiac," which means the "zoo path." This is the root of the word "zodiac" and can be readily interpreted as "the circle of the animals or path of the animals." All but one of the zodiacal constellations is an animal-like being. That exception is Libra (scale).

The Persians named the four royal Persian stars. They are located near each of the cardinal positions that the sun was at on the solstice and equinox around five thousand years ago.

Fig. 2-3.

The Persians documented the first understanding of the four royal Persian stars. We know this because they incorporated the four zodiacal signs into their sculptures and mythology. Other cultures most likely understood this information long before that time, but it wasn't until about three thousand years ago that a representation of the four royal Persian stars was created. This was kind of a golden age when they realized the importance of this information and the sun was in front of those stars. This method of using the sun to inform people of the seasons represented a very reliable calendar.

The sun moves westward 1 degree every 72 years, 2 degrees every 144 years, and 30 degrees every 2,160 years. This is called precession. The Earth's wobble causes it.

Fig. 2-4.

Because of the phenomena of precession, the sun moves westward along the ecliptic continuously. It shifts one degree to the west every seventy-two years, twice the distance of the full moon, which covers a half-degree. The sun precesses 2 degrees to the west every 144 years and 30 degrees to the west (or one zodiacal constellation) every 2,160 years. The slight wobble Earth has around its axis causes this process of precession.

It takes 25, 920 (12 x 2,160) years for the sun to make a complete circuit around the zodiac.

Fig. 2-5.

Every 2,160 years, the sun moves through one complete zodiacal sign, which amounts to 30 degrees. If we multiply that by twelve zodiacal signs, then we can see that it will take 25,920 years for the sun to move through all of the signs and circumnavigate the entire zodiac.

An allegory is a story with a hidden meaning below the surface of the story.

Fig. 2-6.

An allegory is a story with a deeper meaning beneath the surface. For example, the story of Jesus Christ can be looked at as an allegory of the sun's annual journey around the zodiac, something deeper than just the story of a person's life.

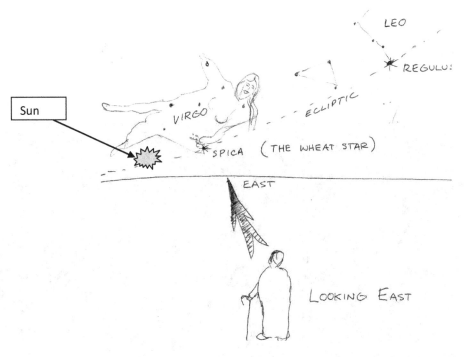

Fig. 2-7 Simple sun/star observing

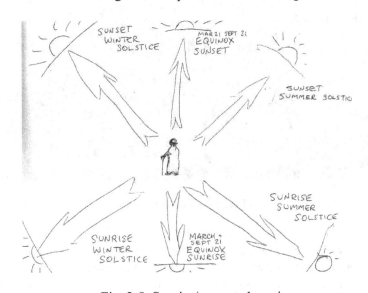

Fig. 2-8. Sunrise/ sunset observing

How did they know what constellation the sun was in a long time ago? They would see a bright star and measure using a divider to note where the sun was. From then on, they could refer to the measurement and know exactly when and what constellation the sun would be in.

Chapter 3

The Four Royal Persian Stars

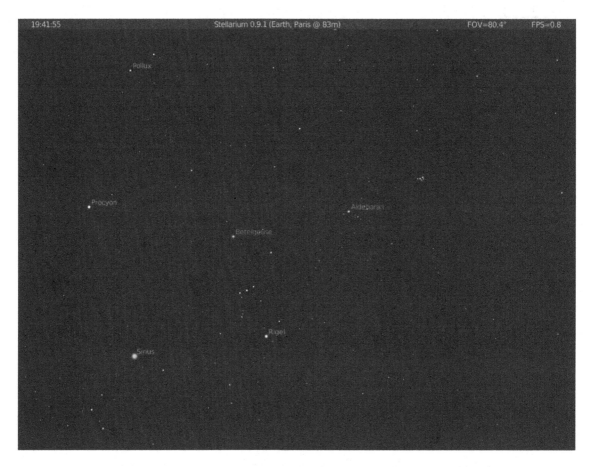

Fig. 3-1. The night sky.

From the earliest times, whether it be one thousand to three million years ago, the night sky has intrigued humans. Today, we are no different than they were. They looked up at it and gasped at its beauty and wonder. So do we. The difference is that they had so little information to go on as to what those tiny twinkling lights in the night were. So they did the best they could to explain it. Human beings have always seen shapes and figures that remind them of something else they know. Therefore, they began to remember these shapes by telling stories.

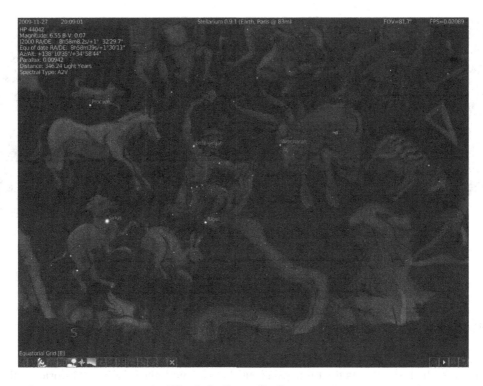

Fig. 3-2. Constellations

Humans began to recognize shapes that reminded them of their natural world and the far reaches of their imagination. This is where the constellations began. The figure of Orion seems to emerge out of the shape of that constellation. However, every culture worldwide sees a different pattern to constellations. For instance, in Japan, the constellation that the Greeks called Orion is believed to be a kimono held at arm's length. In Egypt, it was Osiris. To the Native Americans, it was visualized as a canoe about to enter the Milky River. To the right of Orion is a bull-like shape. The Greeks eventually know this charging bull as Taurus, which means "bull." A little farther to the right is a lamb. This is Aries the Ram/Lamb.

The zodiac is the path that the sun and planets follow along the ecliptic. The sun takes one year to move through all twelve signs of the zodiac, which are as follows, starting from the left, Leo, Cancer, Gemini, Taurus, Aries, Pisces, Aquarius, Capricorn, Sagittarius, Scorpio, Libra, and Virgo.

Fig. 3-3. The zodiac.

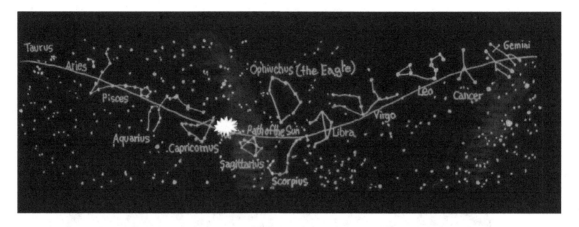

Fig. 3-4. The sun's path along the zodiac.

The sun is shown to the left of Sagittarius and the right of Capricorn. This is where the sun was two thousand years ago on December 21, the winter solstice. Look right and above the sun and note the addition of the constellation Ophiuchus. It is located just above Scorpius. Ophiuchus is the constellation that Middle Eastern cultures interpreted as an eagle.

The zodiacal constellations were created at least twenty-six thousand years ago. The twelve signs of the zodiac are Leo the Lion, Cancer the Crab, Gemini the Twins, Taurus the Bull, Aries the Ram, Pisces the Fish, Aquarius the Man with the Water Jar, Capricorn the Sea Goat, Sagittarius the Archer, Scorpio the Scorpion, Libra the Scales, and Virgo the Virgin. Each sign was invented long ago to explain something about the seasons where they were created, namely in Persia. About twenty-six thousand years ago, the constellations of the zodiac were already established. Many scholars, especially Arthur Harding, agree upon this. "The signs and the constellations of the zodiac coincided with 300 BC and also 26,000 BC. We know they were in use before 300 BC. They must, therefore have been invented not later than 26,000 BC. This gives us some information as to how long man has been studying the stars." (Professor Arthur Harding, *Astronomy* 252)

Five thousand years ago, the zodiacal signs were well known and being used in all of the bull-related religions throughout the Mediterranean, Africa, and Persia. Perhaps the sacred cows of India are a remnant of that ancient era of bull worship. The fact that the zodiacal signs and the seasons of the year fit perfectly with the seasons in Persia of five thousand years ago is additional evidence. The sun takes twenty-six thousand years to make a complete circuit of the zodiac, and it must have already completed that five thousand years ago because the rainy season in November was when the sun was in Capricorn, followed by the rains of December when the sun was in Aquarius and Pisces in January. Then in February, Aries, it was time for the lambs to be born. They celebrated this by putting the occasion into the sky. The same was done in March, the sun was in Taurus, and the bulls were out eating grass in the spring, and the people might have seen more of them and remembered this.

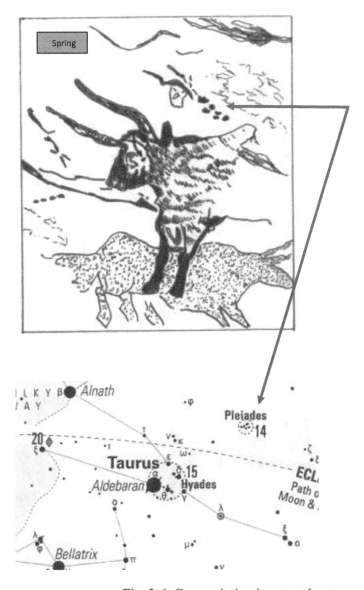

Fig. 3-6. Cave painting is a star chart

On the upper left is a cave painting from seventeen thousand years ago in Lascaux, France. It is of a steer or bull on the ceiling of the cave, and it is painted with very long horns. Above the back of the bull are six stars that are arranged in much the same pattern as the Pleiades star cluster. Compare it to the star chart on the right. It would be an amazing coincidence if this isn't a depiction of the constellation of Taurus. On the upper right, see that the Pleiades is located in approximately the correct area as the cave painting. The horns of the bull appear to be long like those in the constellation, and the V shape of the sideviewing head is like that of the Hyades cluster. If it were painted in 15,000 BC, like the historians say, and it is Taurus, then we can acknowledge that the other constellations of the zodiac were also already named.

17

Here is an ancient Native American pictograph located at North Hedman Lake in the boundary waters of Minnesota. It could be an ancient astronomical depiction. On the left, it could be the "shaman," which looks like the constellation of Orion. Above him are the seven dashes of the Pleiades, and above that are the three "spirit canoes" of the Milky Way. There is a large X on the top, which could be the supernova of 1054 or Capella. Below "Orion," there appears to be a fox, which could be like Lepus. The moose could be Eridanus or Pegasus. The red line below it all is the horizon.

Fig. 3-7. The Hedman Lake shaman (Photo credit to Bob King).

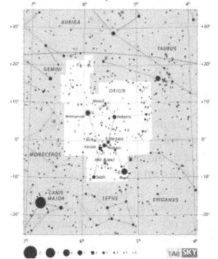

Fig. 3-8. A map of Orion and Taurus.

Let's go back five thousand years ago to the constellation of the bull.

Fig. 3-9. Spring, 3000 BC (Stellarium).

Here we have a rendition of where the sun would be located on March 21, 3000 BC, the vernal equinox/first day of spring. The sun was directly in the head of Taurus the Bull and covering the star Aldebaran. Also note the green square to the right of the word "spring." This light-green S will appear throughout the book. It means spring.

The sun is in Leo on June 21, 3000 BC, the summer solstice.

Summer! SR

Fig. 3-10. Summer, 3000 BC (Stellarium)

In this depiction, we see the second royal Persian star when it is the first day of summer on June 21, 3000 BC. The sun is located in the constellation of Leo the Lion. It is covering the star Regulus, or Rex the Kingly Star. This date is the summer solstice. This is as far north as the sun will travel. The northern hemisphere will receive the maximum amount of sunlight/daylight on this date. The nights are very short in comparison. Note the dark-green SR to the right of "summer."

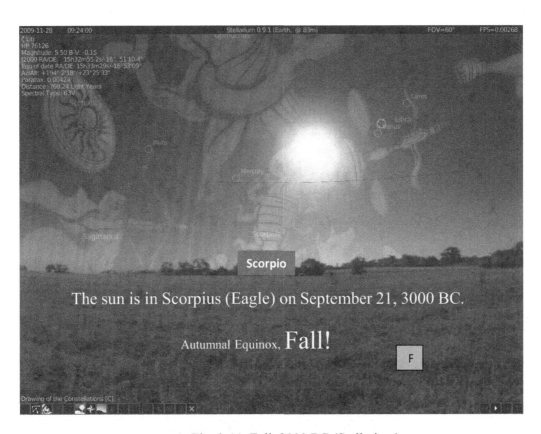

Fig. 3-11. Fall, 3000 BC (Stellarium)

Now look to the right of the word "Fall." An orange F will connote September 21, the first day of fall. The artist depiction shows the sun is in the sign of Scorpio the Scorpion on this date and it is covering the star Antares. The constellation above Scorpio was known as the Eagle. Note a man holding a snake, Oephiucus, the serpent bearer. The ancients believed he was an eagle, not a man, and the eagle held the snake in his beak and thus is the third royal Persian star.

Fig. 3-12. Winter, 3000 BC (Stellarium).

The sun covers the fourth royal Persian star on December 21, 3000 BC, the winter solstice, first day of winter. This is the longest night of the year. The daylight is very short in the Northern Hemisphere. The sun would be located in the constellation of Aquarius and not far from the star Fomalhaut. Note the light-blue W to the right of "winter." Aquarius was shown as a man holding a water jar, and he is dumping out the water toward Pisces.

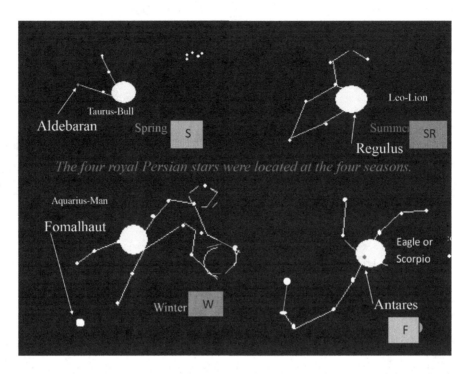

Fig. 3-13. The four seasons.

In this image, note all of the colored seasons around the zodiac. The light-green S on the upper left is spring. On the upper right are the dark-green squares of summer. On the lower right is the orange square of fall. The blue one of winter is in the lower left. When the sun was in those four positions in the sky, and depending upon which of the constellations it was covering, it would determine the time of year it was.

Now we bring them all together and see how they make up the four royal Persian stars. Starting with the light-green square of March 21, the vernal equinox, the sun would be in Taurus near the star Aldebaran. Next, the dark-green SR is on June 21, the summer solstice. The sun would be covering Leo the Lion and Regulus. Then down to the orange F and on the autumnal equinox, September 21, the sun would be covering Antares in Scorpio, or as some cultures called it, the Eagle. Finally, the blue W on December 21, the winter solstice, the sun would be covering Aquarius and near Fomalhaut. Those are the four royal Persian stars and their constellations.

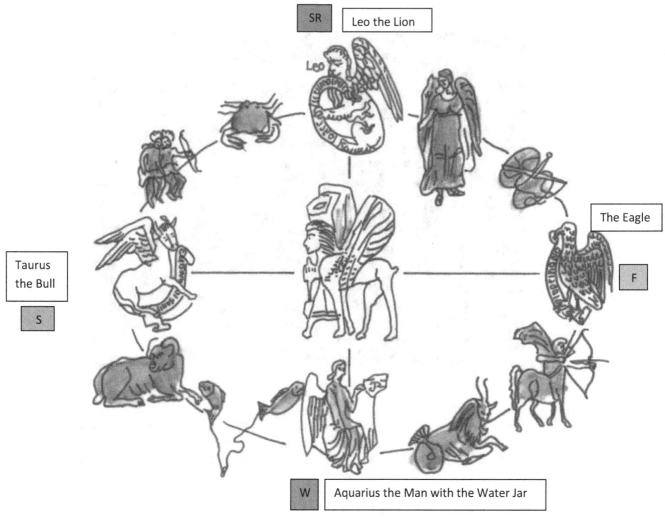

SR | Leo the Lion

The Eagle

F

Taurus the Bull

S

W | Aquarius the Man with the Water Jar

Fig. 3-14. The angels of the zodiac.

We can see how those four royal Persian stars fit into the zodiac.[14] They are located 90 degrees from each other. In this depiction, Taurus and spring (S) are on the far left. Working clockwise, we then see Leo on top as summer (SR), the Eagle on the right as fall (F), and Aquarius on the bottom as winter (W). The other zodiacal signs are all filled in.

Notice the cherub in the middle. It is a composite of the four royal Persian star symbols. The head/face of the cherub is that of a man (Aquarius the Man with the Water Jar.) The cherub has wings like an eagle (the Eagle). It has the body of a lion (Leo the Lion) and the feet of a bull (Taurus the Bull). Thus, the cherub incorporates all of the four seasons into itself.

---

[14] www.mt.net/~watcher/newun.html, the zodiac, cherubims, and the sphinx

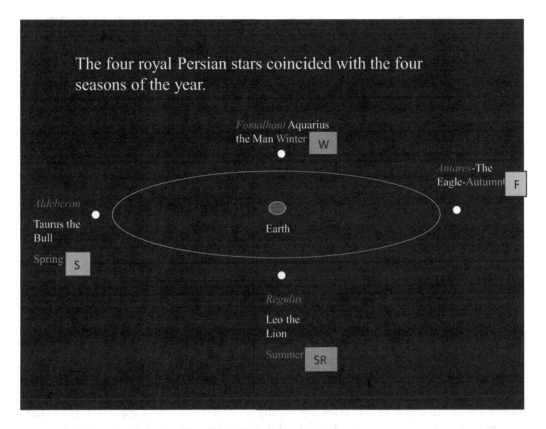

The four royal Persian stars coincided with the four seasons of the year.

Fig. 3-15. The four seasons.

The four royal Persian stars coincided with the four seasons of the year five thousand years ago. In this depiction, it shows Earth in the middle. Of course, Earth is not in the middle of the solar system. This is used only to illustrate that it appears as if the four royal Persian stars move around our planet. These days, we know Earth turns and it is in orbit around the sun, thus accounting for the changing views of the night sky.

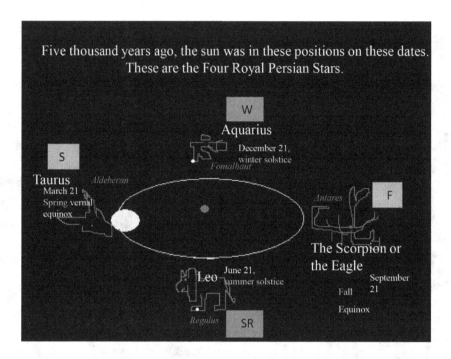

Fig. 3-16. The symbols of the seasons.

　　Here we see another apparent misnomer of Earth in the middle and the sun orbiting Earth, but remember it is only from our earthly point of view that it appears as if the sun orbits around the zodiac when, in fact, Earth's orbit around the sun causes these changes.

　　The important thing to understand is that, when the sun was covering any of the four royal Persian stars, it would help the ancients know the exact date of year. This was a very useful calendar and more reliable than the moon was or any other method available to them.

Chapter 4

The Four Royal Stars Become Integrated into Art and Religion

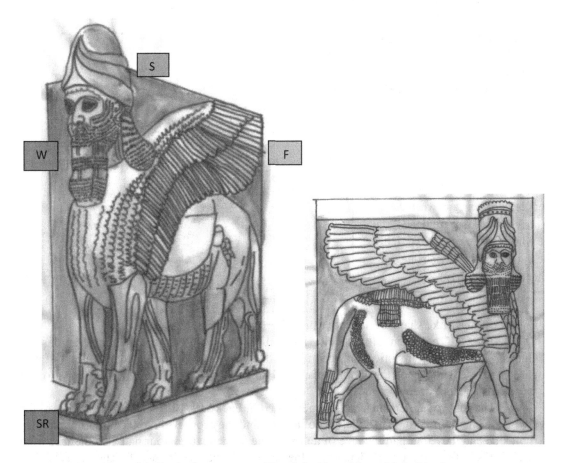

Fig. 4-1. Cherubim with lion's feet.   Fig. 4-2. Cherubim with bull's feet.

This sketch on the left is of a cherubim from the British Museum. The sculpture was carved out of rock in Persia around 900 BC. It was quite common to see these figures throughout ancient Persia. The figure suggests the combination of all four royal Persian stars combined into one. It has the head/face of a man (Aquarius) at the W, the horns of a bull on the head (Taurus) at the S, the wings of an eagle (the Eagle) at the F, and the body and feet of a lion (Leo the Lion) at the SR. Thus, it brings all of the four seasons and the sun's annual journey into one combined symbol. The sketch on the right is another version of a winged bull. It has a face of a man, the horns and hooves of a bull, the wings of an eagle, the tassels or mane of a lion, and a body similar to a lion.

The four royal Persian stars are
mentioned in the Old Testament.

As for the likeness of their faces, the
cherubim's, they had the **face of a
man**; and they four had the face of **a
lion** on the right side; and they four
had the face of **an ox** on the left side;
they four had also the face of **an
eagle.** (Ezekiel 1:10)

As for their rims, they were high and
dreadful, and they four had their rims
full of eyes all about. And when the
living creatures went, the wheels
went beside them; and when the
living creatures rose from the earth,
the wheels rose … for the spirit of
the living creatures was in the
wheels. (Ezekiel 1:19)

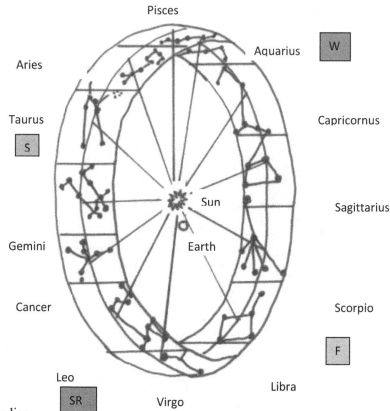

Fig. 4-3. Wheel-like shape of the zodiac.

The Old Testament tells us a clue about the four royal Persian stars/constellations. In
Genesis 3:24, they are mentioned as cherubim. "He drove out the men; and at the east of the
garden of Eden, he placed the cherubim and a flaming sword which turned every way, to guard
the way to the tree of life."

The four royal Persian stars are mentioned in Ezekiel 1:10. "As for the likeness of their
faces, the cherubim's, they had the face of a man, and they four had the face of a lion on the
right side and they four had the face of an ox on the left side, they four had also the face of an
eagle." These four figures are identical to the ancient Persian sculpture of a cherub that
combined the same composites into one sculpture as in Fig. 4-1 and 4-2.

A little farther in Ezekiel 11:19, we read, "As for their rims, they were high and
dreadful, and they four had their rims full of eyes all about. And when the living creatures
went, the wheels went beside them; and when the living creatures rose from the earth, the
wheels rose … for the spirit of the living creatures was in the wheels."

This is a fairly vivid idea about the movement of the zodiac being suggested as likened
to the movement of a wheel. The rim of the wheel is like the ecliptic, the path the sun follows
every year. The wheel rises during the night, and the zodiacal creatures have "eyes" upon it
that look down upon us. Then the zodiacal signs move westward. As it reads, the living
creatures went, and then they rise again. And if one personifies them, then they appear to have
a spirit.[15]

---

[15] Arthur Harding, *Astronomy*, 255.

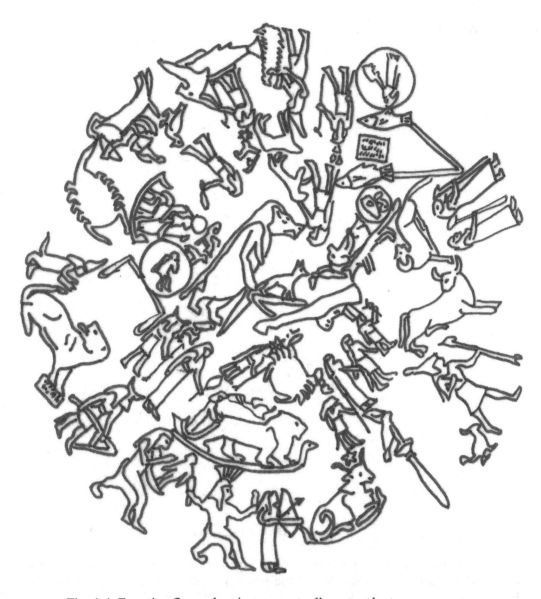

Fig. 4-4. Egyptian figure drawings are actually a star chart.

    This is a drawing on a ceiling in an Egyptian burial tomb discovered in Egypt. It is dated from around 800 BC. At first, it looks like a hodgepodge of creatures all drawn in a spiral-like pattern.[16]

[16] "The Zodiac of Dendera," www.lindahall.org/events_exhib/exhibit/exhibits/.../zodiac_dendera.shtm...

Fig. 4-5. Dendera star chart.

　　　A closer look reveals it is a star chart. Many of the same ancient constellations as those of the Persians are depicted here. Plus, there are a few contrary ones. On the far right side is the light-green S near the Bull of Heaven, Taurus. Then we look near the lower middle and see the dark-green SR connoting summer. And above it is Leo the Lion. Moving left to the nine o'clock position, we see the orange F of Scorpio. This view does show a scorpion. Near the top and slightly right is the light-blue W of Aquarius. Of interest is that the North Star would be located by the wolf's nose. This would be the end of the handle of the Little Dipper, Ursa Minor. The Greek influence on our constellations was powerful. They admired bears, and that is why the great bears are located in the northern skies. To the Egyptians, who had no bears, this would be unheard of. That is why they have a hippo and mooring post where the Greeks saw Ursa Major, the Great Bear.

Father Time, Aeon, surrounded with the zodiac and the four seasons, AD 100.

Fig. 4-6. The Greek god Aeon.

The ancient Greeks personified time as a young man, who they called Aeon or Father Time. He was also known as Cronos or Saturn, the namesake of Saturnalia, celebrated on December 25. Here he is with the four seasons and mother earth. Spring is the nymph on the far left. Then to the right is summer, autumn, mother earth, and the nymph of winter on the far right. The figure of Aeon is surrounded with the zodiac. Near his hand and the S is Taurus with a bull figure. Below the S, we see the Twins of Gemini, Cancer the Crab, Leo the Lion (SR) above the nymph of spring, and Virgo the Virgin below Aeon's foot.

Then above the S, things get a little in disarray. These were complex topics even to the ancients. It appears to be Pisces and then Aquarius near the light-blue W. Then there is Capricorn. On the bottom of the opposite side, just above the middle nymphs (autumn's) head appears to be Libra and then Aries. This would be out of order. Then there is Sagittarius. Then above that is the Scorpion of Scorpius by the F.

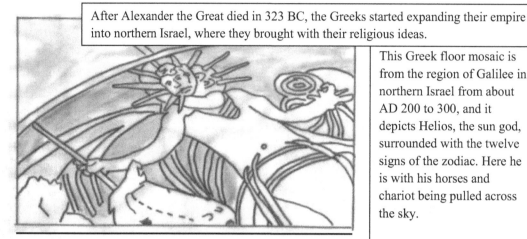

This Greek floor mosaic is from the region of Galilee in northern Israel from about AD 200 to 300, and it depicts Helios, the sun god, surrounded with the twelve signs of the zodiac. Here he is with his horses and chariot being pulled across the sky.

Fig. 4-7. Helios.

Fig. 4-8. A floor mosaic in England.

In the early 1930s, archaeologists in Verulam, England, unearthed a mosaic that depicted a sun god (American Peoples Encyclopedia) that appeared similar to Apollo or the Druid sun god Bel. Other sources believe it is Oceanus or Cerunnos. It does not show the zodiac, but it does have four corners. On four sides, there are wine mugs. Could this be like Dionysus? This floor mosaic demonstrates how far reaching the personification of human deification was. The date of the mosaic was believed to be around AD 160 to 190. Another account tells the town burned in AD 61. It tells us that they were borrowing some ideas from the Middle East via the Roman occupation of Britain in this town, which is north of London.

The Greek influence into Israel from 200 BC to AD 250 brings a merging of cultures.

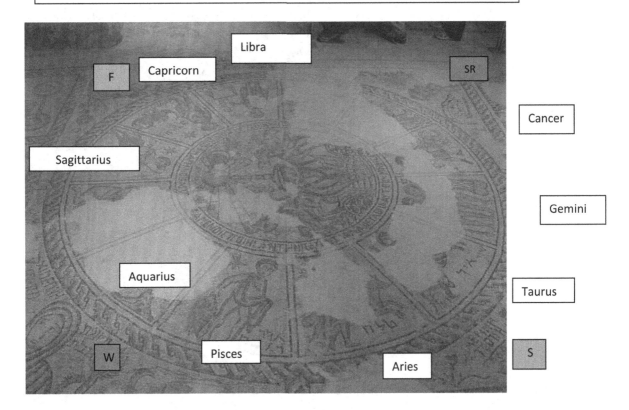

Fig. 4-9. The Sepphoris mosaic.

Here is an ancient floor mosaic from Sepphoris of AD 200, near Nazareth in Israel. In the middle, we see a depiction of a Helios-like object with rays going out from it. Four horses are pulling the sun, and little wheels are on a cart. We can also see, starting from the lower right, the springtime depiction of a young woman and lilies of spring, and we still celebrate Easter lilies today. There is also some Greek writing in this mosaic. Above it, along the zodiacal signs is Hebrew writing. This tells us there was some kind of cultural exchange going on between Greeks and Hebrews. They were borrowing information. The lower right area has the light-green S of spring with some remaining bull-like drawings upon the zodiacal circle in the tile work. This is Taurus. Moving above it toward the dark-green SR is another woman, slightly older than the first, and she has a sickle and some other tools for plants. Next to her is Leo the Lion. The upper left is a depiction of a middle-aged woman with fruits. This is the time of the year of the harvest. She is standing near to the Scorpion at the F. This is Scorpius. Then to the bottom left side, we see an older woman all bundled up because she is elderly, like the year is old. It is winter, and she has some grains and perhaps a flame of fire. To her right is where Aquarius would be, but it is damaged. We see the W of winter in this area, and to the right is where Pisces is located. So, here is an ancient anthropomorphized idea, a pre-Christian myth about the seasons of the year, the sun's journey, and the zodiacal signs. It is an immersion of Hellenistic ideas and Hebrew writing. Most likely, there was a mixing of traditions and some new interpretations of the sun, the zodiac, and the four seasons.

Fig. 4-10. A sun god.

In the middle of the Sepphoris mosaic is a cartoon-like sun god depiction. It shows the four horses pulling the sun and the wheels of his chariot. Nearest to the emblem is writing in Hebrew. Outside of the emblem is writing in Greek. Greek ideas that a god is likened to the bright rays of the sun and pulled on a chariot by a team of four horses could be the origins of generating new notions and ideas about religious practice in Israel.

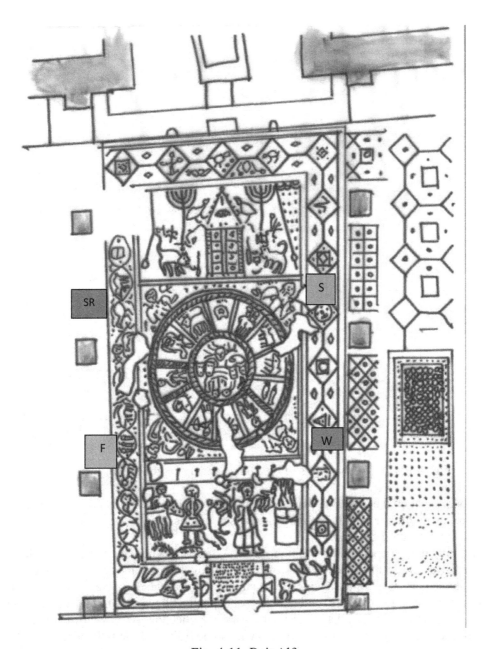

Fig. 4-11. Beit Alfa.

This Hellenistic Jew floor mosaic from AD 250 near Galilee is at Beit Alfa and is from an old Jewish synagogue. In the center is a Helios-like sun god pulled by four horses. We can see the menorah symbols near the top area and the bay where the Ark of the Covenant was kept. There is a zodiac wheel in the middle and the same signs of the zodiac we know today. Below the zodiac wheel is the story of Abraham about to slay his son Isaac. This is a perfect example of the merger of these two cultures.

Fig. 4-12. The twelve signs of the zodiac and a sun god.

Zooming in on the central zodiac wheel at Beit Alfa in northern Israel, we can see the Helios-like sun god in the middle with his four horses and his chariot. He has a few stars around him and the crescent moon.

Starting in the upper right is the light-green S of spring with a woman figure below it. She has a flower-like shape to her right. Move down below her onto the zodiac and see Taurus the Bull; above it are Gemini the Twins. On the upper left near the dark-green SR is what looks like a young woman, a young bird, and perhaps some plants. She is near to the zodiacal sign of Leo the Lion, and to the left of that is Virgo the Virgin. Notice the Hebrew writing. On the lower left near the orange F is a young woman with some fruits and the fall zodiacal symbol of Scorpios. Then onward to the lower right near the blue W is a middle-aged woman who has some grains and the zodiacal sign of Aquarius. Note the woman in the upper right looks older, and this might be because the ancients considered March the end of the yearly cycle.

36

Abraham's journey is like the sun's motion.

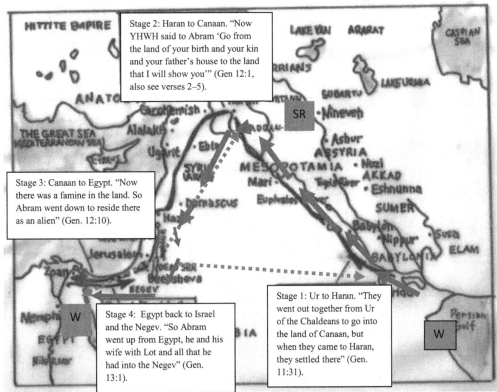

Stage 2: Haran to Canaan. "Now YHWH said to Abram 'Go from the land of your birth and your kin and your father's house to the land that I will show you'" (Gen 12:1, also see verses 2–5).

Stage 3: Canaan to Egypt. "Now there was a famine in the land. So Abram went down to reside there as an alien" (Gen. 12:10).

Stage 4: Egypt back to Israel and the Negev. "So Abram went up from Egypt, he and his wife with Lot and all that he had into the Negev" (Gen. 13:1).

Stage 1: Ur to Haran. "They went out together from Ur of the Chaldeans to go into the land of Canaan, but when they came to Haran, they settled there" (Gen. 11:31).

Fig. 4-13. The route of Abraham.

Ab –Ra-Ham. In Hebrew, Ab means "father." Ra was the ancient Egyptian sun god. Ham means "hot," or it also was the name of one of Noah's sons. Therefore, Ab-ra-ham could mean "Father-Sun-hot." Or it can mean the "son of Noah." He is considered to be the father of the Jews. **When we look at Abraham's journey from the perspective of Jerusalem, he follows the path of the sun during the year.** The "sun" rises in the direction of Ur on December 21, moves north to Haran on June 21, then heads south to Egypt, and sets in this location on December 21. Abraham then moves back north to Jerusalem in spring. *www.abarimpublications.com

Abraham was a keeper of bulls. He is like the sun moving out of the zodiacal sign of the Bull of Taurus and into the lamb sign of Aries. This Cigoli painting shows Abraham about to sacrifice his son Isaac. Instead, he sacrifices the ram.

Fig. 4-14. Abraham is about to slay his son Isaac but instead slays a ram in the thicket.

Fig. 4-15. Abraham slays a ram.

Here is the entryway to the ancient synagogue of Beit Alfa. It shows some Hebrew and Greek writing on the floor. This is the Genesis 18–22 story of Abraham. Note the bull on the right and the lion on the left flank of the entryway. Abraham is the figure with the long knife. He holds Isaac, whom he is about to slay and offer as a sacrifice to God, in his other hand. The flaming altar is on the far right. Just to the left of Abraham's head is the hand of God descending from the heavens, and it says, "Do not lay your hand on the lad or do anything to him. Kill the ram in the bush instead." So that is what Abraham does. He kills the ram as a sacrifice. On the left side are two figures with a donkey, and this is what is described in the story as they witnessed the event. What does this story tell us? It says Abraham was the keeper of bulls and the bull era was over. He did not kill his son. Instead, he kills a ram, and he transformed Isaac into the Age of the Ram. He sacrificed the ram over his firstborn son. Abraham becomes like a sun god devouring the signs of the zodiac.

Perhaps the most important thing to come out of Beit Alfa is the coming together of Hellenistic and Hebrew ideas. This is a synagogue, obviously a place sacred to Hebrews. Yet it has Greek writing and sun god symbology. The two seem to be merging and satisfying the need to pool together two distinct cultures into one monotheism. There are no Christian symbols on this mosaic at all. It is as if Christianity had not yet been invented when this was built in AD 250, or perhaps Beit Alfa was an attempt to create a new religion that did bring together Old Testament ideas along with Greek sun god and zodiac beliefs.

Fig. 4-16. Tiberius mosaic.

Another synagogue mosaic to inspect is at Tiberius, Israel, again near the Sea of Galilee. It is dated to around AD 300. At the top, one can see the two menorahs; thus, it is definitely a Hebrew place of worship. Once again, there are no Christian icons or resemblances anywhere. The date of AD 300 is a full 270 years of development after Christ's death. The writing along the zodiac is in Hebrew. In the middle of the mosaic is a sun god-like figure, a young man with the rays of the sun jutting out in multiple directions. He holds a globe or the moon in his hand. Below him might have been a chariot and the four horses, but a seventh-century wall built over the top of the mosaic damaged them. Surrounding the sun god are the twelve signs of the zodiac.

We can start in the upper left at the light-green S and a depiction of spring. It shows a young man with some plant-like items. The constellation to his right is Taurus. So we are in the sign of spring. Then to the lower left and the dark-green SR, we see a fellow with a crown (Dionysus). He has a sickle in his hand and again some produce. Above him and to his upper right is Leo the Lion (S). To the lower right side and above the orange F icon, we see a sharp-looking fellow with grapes and a glass of wine. Possibly Bacchus? His sign is Scorpio. Finally on the upper right is the wintertime man, and he is near the blue W of Aquarius. Here we complete the cycle of the four seasons and the harvesting of grapes.

Fig. 4-17. A youthful sun god.

     This close-up of the sun god shows his halo and the rays around his head. He is youthful with blushed cheeks. He has his right hand raised in a "follow me" fashion. The globe in his left hand almost appears to look like a crescent moon with earth shine, but it was possibly a mirror. He also holds a whip or flail. Hebrew writing was around the zodiac above his head.

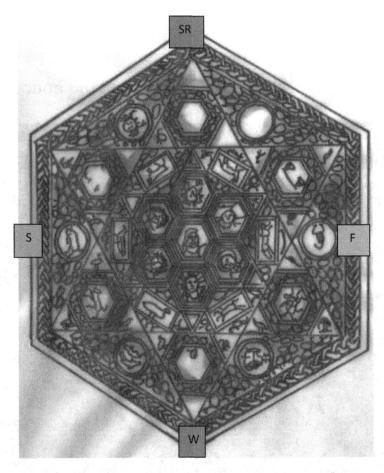

Fig. 4-18. Yet another floor mosaic dated from between AD 100 and 250 in Tunisia at Bir Chana.

It shows a Star of David shape. The zodiac runs around the perimeter, and each constellation is with a circle. You can see the bull on the left at S and the scorpion at the right at F. And the other two royal Persian star constellations of Aquarius at W and Leo at SR are hard to see, but they can be interpreted by the surrounding constellations.

What is really interesting is in the middle of this mosaic. In the very center, we see a figure with a sickle, Saturn. Remember in Greek mythology that Saturn was considered to be Father Time/Cronus. Below Saturn is Apollo, the sun god. Above Saturn is Mercury with his little wings on the sides of his head. To the left of Mercury, we see Jupiter wearing a king's crown. Below Jupiter is the lovely Venus. Go back up to the top figure of Mercury, and to his right, we see a soldier with a spear, Mars. Below Mars is the moon.

Now, find all the days of the week. Let's start with the bottom figure, the sun, and move counterclockwise around to each figure. You will see the seven days of the week: Sunday (sun), Monday (moon), Tuesday (Mars, named after Teu the Teutonic god of war), Wednesday (named after Woden or Mercury), Thursday (named after Thor or Jupiter), Friday (named after Freya or Venus), and into the middle is Saturn for Saturday. To think these Greek ideas are incorporated into a Jewish symbol demonstrates the melting pot of two cultures.

Chapter 5

The Four Royal Persian Stars Become the Four Archangels

Fig. 5-1. Twinkling stars.

Our ancestors of twenty thousand years ago tried to explain the natural world in whatever ways they could. When they looked at stars, they noticed they twinkled. Somebody back then must have wondered why this occurred. It seems probable that they believed stars twinkled because they had wings, thus the beginning construct of angels. They appeared to be tiny far away but moving across the sky. These tiny winged creatures were called ang-els, an Arabic word that means "messengers of god."

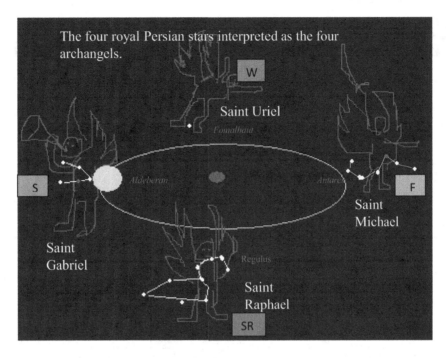

Fig. 5-2. The four archangels.

The concept of stars twinkling is incorporated into the four royal Persian stars and their transformation into the four archangels. The trumpeting angel on the left near the light-green S is Gabriel. This is like the horn of Taurus. He blows through the horn and announces upcoming events. The summer angel on the bottom near the dark-green SR is Raphael. He has the word Ra in his name, which means "sun" in Egyptian. Because the sun is at its highest and hottest in the summer, this seems fitting to call this position Ra. The angel of fall is on the right, near the orange F, and it is Saint Michael. He is depicted with a sword and shield. He is very soldier like. It is possible that, when the sun is located near the star Antares in the fall, this was interpreted as warlike. Antares is a word passed down from the Greeks, and it means "anti-Aries" or "rival of Mars." To the Greeks, Aries was the war god Mars. Because Antares and Mars are very similar in color, it could be that the ancients thought they were very much alike and were rivals. The final angel is Uriel, at the top near the blue W. This angel is known to have water symbology involved with it. Ur was a city that was near a river or the sea in ancient times. Perhaps this association with water and because the sun is in Aquarius at winter is the reason for this.

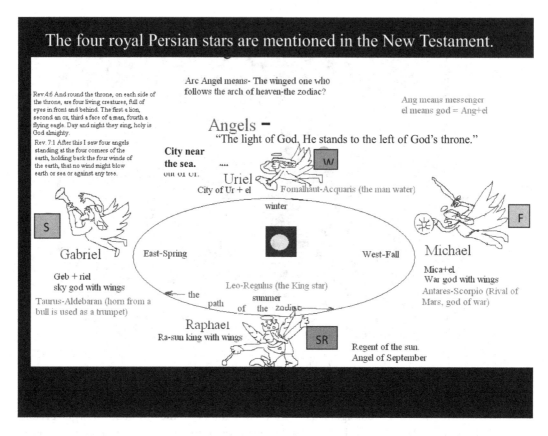

Fig. 5-3. Seasons and the angels.

The New Testament association with the Four Royal Stars can be found in Revelation-4:6. "And round the throne, on each side of the throne, are four living creatures, full of eyes in front and behind. The first a lion, the second an ox, third a face of a man, fourth a flying eagle. Day and night they sing holy is God almighty." The last verse gives one the impression that they are angelic because they sing holy songs. Then in Revelation 7:1, we read, "After this I saw four angels standing at the four corners of the earth, holding back the four winds of the earth, that no wind might blow earth or sea or against any tree." The very idea of four angels at four corners sounds like an association with the four cardinal directions or the four points of the zodiac.

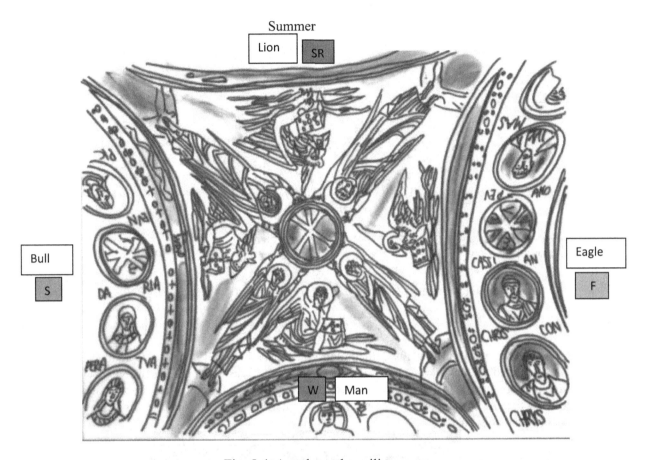

Fig. 5-4. Angels on the ceiling.

Here we can see on this chapel ceiling from Ravenna, Italy, an association of angels and the four royal Persian stars. On the left side is the icon S of spring, and we see a winged bull or ox. At the top is the SR and a winged lion of summer. On the right side is the F and an eagle. On the bottom is the W and the winged man of winter.

Also, notice the similarity to the central symbol of the X shape and the crux or Stonehenge-like shape. This is a symbol of the four seasons.

Fig. 5-5. Winged cherubim as angels.

On the portal of Chartres Cathedral in France is a thousand-year-old depiction of Jesus with a halo and rays around his head. He sits on a throne. Below him are the twelve disciples (three of whom are cut off in the photo). Around the Christ are the four royal Persian stars now shown as angelic cherubs. They are pretty clear to interpret as angels, and the wings on these creatures can be seen.

Fig. 5-6. St. Michael.

At St. Michael's Church in Duluth, Minnesota, is a stained glass window with St. Michael upon it. He is very warlike in this depiction, holding a sword in one hand and a shield in the other. His wings are white and on either side of his head. Remember, in the fall, the sun would be covering Antares, which means anti-Ares, or Mars, thus the warlike depiction of St. Michael

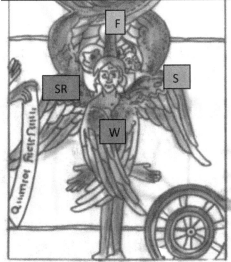

An angel with the face of a man, an ox, a lion, and an eagle

Fig. 5-7. The wheels of the zodiac.　　　Fig. 5-8. The Molten Sea.

The angel on the left is a composite figure with all of the royal Persian stars brought into one. It is not unlike the Persian winged bull that was shown in the British Museum. The center figure has a man's face. To his left is a lion. Above him is the eagle, and to the right is the ox. He stands on a wheel, and the verses of Ezekiel 1:10 can be interpreted into this kind of cherubim. The Molten Sea is shown on the right. It was at Solomon's Temple and is explained below.

Fig. 5-9. Inside Solomon's Temple.

The drawing above shows the most holy of the holies, the sacred interior of the Jewish King Solomon's Temple in Jerusalem. It contained many cherubs inside, especially in the sacred room (on the right) where two large cherubs stood side by side. Those cherubs are described in Kings 6. They have features of a lion, eagle wings, and the face of a man. The entryway also has many cherubs along the wall. These appear to have the features of a lion, man, eagle, and ox. There they are again, the four royal Persian stars. Located just outside of the temple was the Molten Sea with twelve oxen. This was probably used for purification purposes.

47

Chapter 6

The Zodiac Inside of the Holy Roman Catholic Church and St. Peter's in Rome

Roman coin

300 AD Constantine in front of Apollo, the Roman sun god.

Fig. 6-1. Constantine and Apollo.

Now we start to see the coming age of Christianity. The Roman Emperor Constantine in AD 306 can be given a great deal of credit for this. Constantine is depicted in front of Apollo on this gold coin. Constantine was a worshipper of Apollo, the sun god. His mother Helen was a Christian. She supposedly found a piece of the true cross in AD 300 while on a pilgrimage to the Holy Land. Constantine led his army against the Persians in a battle called Mulvan Bridge in AD 323. Before the battle, he had a dream that showed a cross above his army. He had a vision or heard a voice in the dream say, "By this sign, conquer." Therefore, Constantine ordered his men to put cross symbols on their shields and breastplates, and he won the battle. Constantine is said to have converted to Christianity before he died in AD 337.

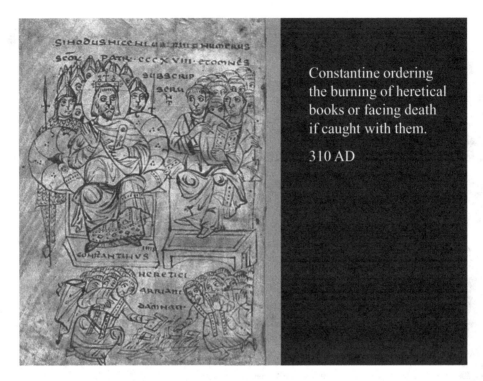

Constantine ordering
the burning of heretical
books or facing death
if caught with them.

310 AD

Fig. 6-2. Constantine's decree.

Around the year AD 310, Constantine ordered a decree that all heretical books and papers be brought to him and burned. If anyone were caught with heretical items, he or she faced death. This was a very stern warning to abide or die. The drawing shows a halo around Constantine's head and also a crux and crown atop him. His soldiers also have cruxes on their swords, while the pagans' heretics on the right have no such Christian iconography.

Fig. 6-3. Constantine and Sol Invicta.

This Roman coin from AD 309 or 310 is dedicated to Constantine and shows Sol Invicta on the right side. Constantine must have switched from a Sol Invicta sun worshipper to a Jesus worshipper before he died.

A. Neros Arena   B. Divider   C. Obelisk   D. Temple to the Unknown God
E. Corner   F. Outerwall   G. Grandstand   H. Concessions   I. Turret.   J.
Helios Statue   K. Main Entrance   L. Shops   M. Temple to Apollo   N.
Temple to Mars   O. Oak Tree   P. Memoria Toromulus   Q. Campi Trianfali
R. Monte Vaticano   S. Village of Barbarini and house of Sarno

Circus of Nero

Fig. 6-4. Circus of Nero.

While Constantine was emperor, some very radical changes came to Rome. He ordered the demolition of the ancient Circus of Nero. Caligula originally built this structure in AD 50 to have chariot races and other sporting events. You can see the structure had an obelisk in the middle of it, which the Egyptians originally made in Heliopolis around 1000 BC. It most likely was an item of Roman bootie from war. Some documents say it was set up in front of Apollo's temple to work as a sun dial or sun pillar. The dome-shaped structure behind the obelisk is the Temple to Apollo, the sun god. The other smaller temple in front of the obelisk was a temple to Mars.

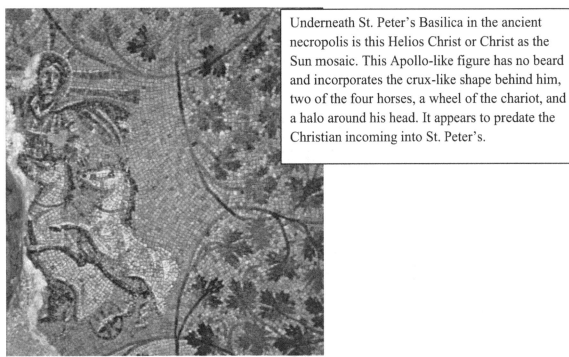

Underneath St. Peter's Basilica in the ancient necropolis is this Helios Christ or Christ as the Sun mosaic. This Apollo-like figure has no beard and incorporates the crux-like shape behind him, two of the four horses, a wheel of the chariot, and a halo around his head. It appears to predate the Christian incoming into St. Peter's.

Fig. 6-5. A sun god under St. Peter's.

Fig. 6-6. Circus of Nero.
In its heyday, this is how Circus of Nero looked with the two turrets in the façade.
There are four horses on each turret. In the middle of the structure is the obelisk.

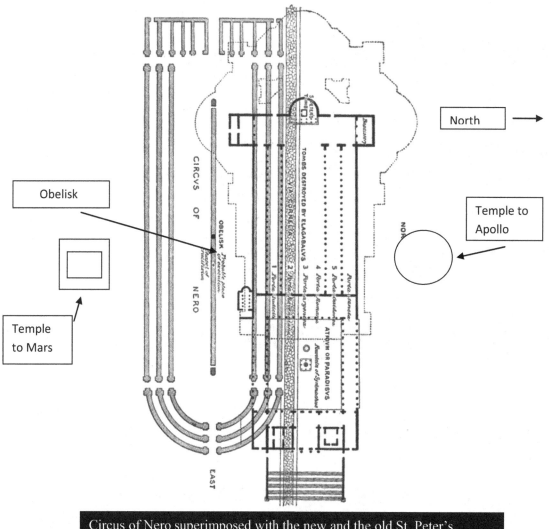

North →

Obelisk

Temple to Apollo

Temple to Mars

Circus of Nero superimposed with the new and the old St. Peter's

Fig. 6-7. Circus of Nero and St. Peter's.

Here is the project that Constantine undertook to revamp the Circus of Nero. This depiction shows the racetrack compared to the first St. Peter's to be built on top. You can see where the obelisk was located at the old site. The Temple of Apollo was located right where it says "North" and the new St. Peter's was constructed. A graveyard to the west of the Temple of Apollo was incorporated into St. Peter's.

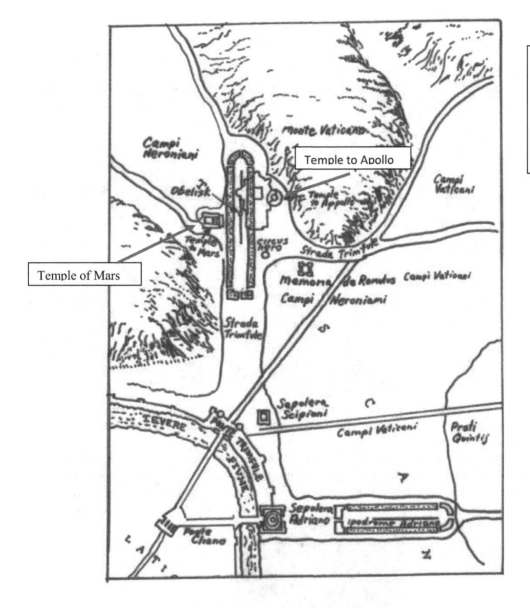

Circus of Nero superimposed with St. Peter's and the old Temples of Mars and Apollo.

Temple to Apollo

Temple of Mars

Fig. 6-8. The layout of St. Peter's.

Here is an overhead view showing the Circus of Nero layout with the Temple of Mars on the left and the Temple of Apollo on the right. The obelisk was left alone at the same site it was on at the Circus of Nero until the sixteenth century when it was painstakingly moved to its present location. Notice the Monte Vaticano behind it. This is where the Vatican namesake originated from. Supposedly, they grew grapes on the Vatican hillside in dedication to Dionysus, the god of wine.

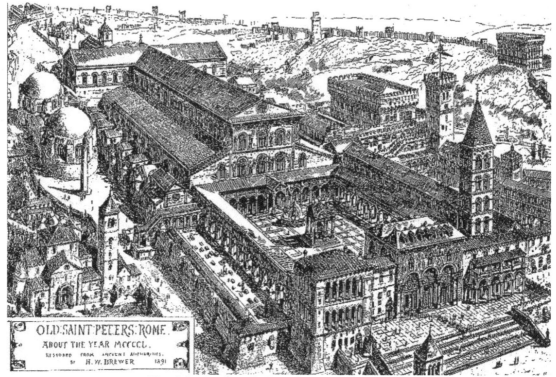

OLD·SAINT·PETERS·ROME·
ABOUT THE YEAR MCCCCL.
RESTORED FROM ANCIENT AUTHORITIES,
BY H. W. BREWER 1891

Fig. 6-9. The first St. Peter's.

Here is the first St. Peter's that Constantine built in AD 320. It still has some resemblance to the old Circus of Nero with the two turrets in the front. You can see the obelisk to the left side of the basilica.

St. Peter's Church was built over the 'site' of the death of St. Peter. He was crucified around AD 67, upside down at the opening to the old catacombs that went underground. The Bible does not mention Peter being in Rome, and the Romans have no record of this occurring either. One of the curious thoughts is that St. Peter was a fisherman, and Jesus said in Matthew 4:19, "Follow me, and I will make you fishers of men."

Fig. 6-10. St. Peter.

Fig. 6-11. Interior view of Old St. Peter's.

Constantine built the first St. Peter's Basilica in AD 320. He had built it right over the top of the razed Temple of Apollo. Here we see an artist's drawing of the first St. Peter's. It was laid out in a crux-like shape. A baldachin was built over St. Peter's tomb, which had four pillars and a dome on top of it. Above the altar of the first St. Peter's was a crux and an inscription that read "*In Excelsios deo et in Terra Pax Homineus.*" Translated, it means "God Almighty of the earth and man." In the middle of that inscription, we see an emblem of Christ with a halo around him and the rays moving out. That is like the sun.

Fig. 6-12. The Old St. Peter's

Are those the four royal Persian stars atop the chapel of the old St. Peter's? In the middle and between the two façade "windows" are the twelve disciples, apparently reading Bibles or singing in a chorus with a cross in the middle. This is like the twelve signs of the zodiac. On each side of the central cross are two angelic figures, a total of four shapes. The figures nearest the crux appear to be lighting the candles.

I am skeptical regarding the following evidence as no real clear drawings nor descriptions of this part of old St. Peter's Basilica have been found to date. Perhaps someone with loads of time can better research this.

If the "puffy-looking figure" on the far left were a lion, then that would be Mark/Leo the Lion. The next angelic figure to the right has what appears to be horns, and this could be Taurus and the S of spring. On the right side of the cross is the man and the blue W, which makes sense to be Aquarius/Matthew. The far right angelic figure near the dark yellow F appears to have birdlike features, and that could be the Eagle or John.

Thus, the four royal Persian stars appear to be laid out from right to left in a correct four seasons order—fall, winter, spring, and summer—upon the façade of the old chapel.

Fig. 6-13. The façade of St. Peter's.

Here, I am in front of the new St. Peter's Basilica, which was built in 1580 and completed around 1620. The obelisk is behind me. Caligula put up that obelisk back in AD 37. It originally stood in the middle of the Circus of Nero and in front of the Temple of Apollo. It was moved in 1586 directly in front of the new St. Peter's. Notice the façade of St. Peter's has two turrets and bears a slight resemblance to the old Circus of Nero.

Fig. 6-14. The Piazza

The obelisk, which originally stood in the Egyptian city of Heliopolis (the city of the sun god Helio) now sits in Rome as a sun dial in the piazza in front of St. Peter's, looking east. Notice the layout of the lines on the pavement is much the same as the Stonehenge arrangement. Lines point to the rising of the summer sun, equinox sun, and winter sun. They also are arranged in the direction of the setting sun on those special dates.

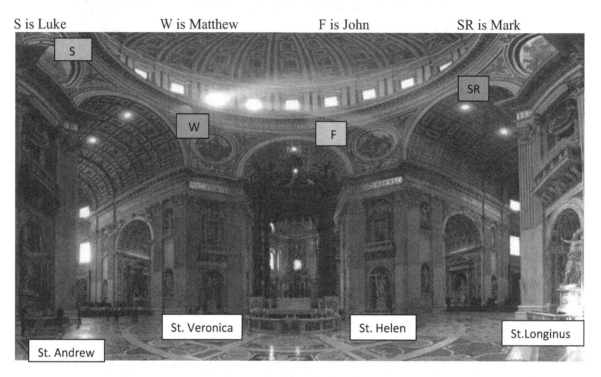

S is Luke   W is Matthew   F is John   SR is Mark

St. Veronica   St. Helen   St.Longinus

St. Andrew

Fig. 6-15. Inside St. Peter's.

       Now we enter into St. Peter's Basilica and go to the central apse where the baldachin is located in the lower center of this photo. On the top of the photo are the four royal Persian star pendentives with S, W, F, and SR colored squares next to them. The baldachin in the center has four pillars and a flat roof with four corners. Notice also the four figures at floor level inset into the major transept supports. On the far left is the figure of Andrew, a disciple of Christ, who was crucified sideways. To the right of Andrew is the figure of Veronica, who supposedly put the veil upon Jesus's face and received a perfect image of him. To the right of the baldachin is the figure of Helen, the mother of Constantine. She holds a crux. The figure on the far right is Longinus, the Roman soldier who thrust a spear or lance into Christ's abdomen, where blood and water poured out. He is shown holding a spear or lance.

       Above the four sculptures are the four medallions or pendentives of the four Gospel writers. We shall start on the far left with the light-green S, Luke. To the right of him and above Veronica is the blue W, Matthew. To his right is John at the orange F and above Helen. The far right figure near the dark-green SR and above Longinus is Mark.

St. Matthew  St. John

St. Veronica   Bernini's sun window   St. Helen

Fig. 6-16. The baldachin and Bernini sun window.

Here is another view of the central apse with the baldachin with the four spiral columns. On the upper left is St. Matthew with the blue W of winter. Matthew is like Aquarius. On the right pendentive is St. John with the orange F of fall. He is like the eagle where later cultures saw it as a serpent held by Ophiucus. In the far middle is the window designed by Bernini, which has the chair of St. Peter incorporated into it. Directly below the F of fall is St. Helen; directly below the W of winter is St. Veronica.

Fig. 6-17. The Baldachin.

Mark is Leo the Lion and summer; Luke is Taurus and spring. Here we can see the top of the baldachin. It has a flat top, four corners, and edges around those corners. An arched roof is on top of the flat top. The vaults support the central gold crux. Alongside the vault are many angelic-like beings, some with wings. We can also see on the left side where St. Mark would be, with the lion of Leo at the SR. To the right is St. Luke with the ox of Taurus and the light-green S. Notice the sunlight pouring in from the south-facing window to the right. It nicely illuminates St. Peter's tomb.

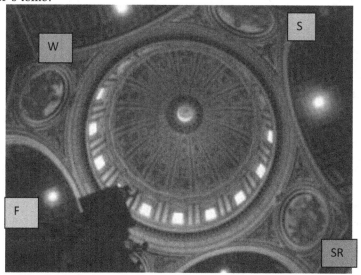

Fig. 6-18. St. Peter's Dome (Photo by Nancy Norland).

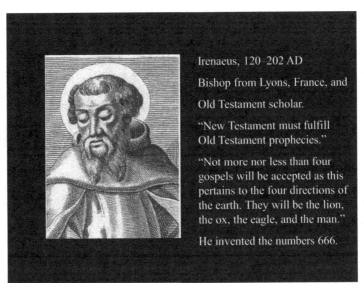

Irenaeus, 120–202 AD

Bishop from Lyons, France, and Old Testament scholar.

"New Testament must fulfill Old Testament prophecies."

"Not more nor less than four gospels will be accepted as this pertains to the four directions of the earth. They will be the lion, the ox, the eagle, and the man."

He invented the numbers 666.

Fig. 6-19. Irenaeus.

St. Irenaeus, a bishop from Lyons, France, and an Old Testament scholar, associated the four Gospel writers with the four royal Persian stars. He wrote *Against Heresies* in which he said, "It is not possible that the Gospels can either be more or fewer in number than they are. For since there are four zones of the world in which we live, and four principal winds, it is fitting that we should have four pillars. The first will be the lion, then the ox, the eagle, and the man." [17] Irenaeus also invented the numbers 666. [18]

St. Mark with the Lion of summer and Leo

SR

Fig. 6-20. St. Mark

St. Mark is shown with the lion. That would be Leo the Lion, and it would be summer.

[17] Irenaus, Against Heresies, Gaul, 180 A.D., Book 3, Chap. 11, 7-9
[18] Irenaeus, Against Heresies, Gaul, 180 A.D. Book 5, Chap. 29-2
www.textexcavation.com/irenaeusah,html

Fig. 6-21.St. Matthew

This is St. Matthew, and he is shown with a little man. This is the equivalent of Aquarius, and it would be winter.

Fig. 6-22. St. John

St. John is shown with an eagle, and this represents fall when the sun was in the Eagle or Scorpius.

St. Luke with the ox or
bull of spring and Taurus

S

Fig. 6-23. St. Luke

The light-green S represents spring, and here we see St. Luke with an ox or a bull. This was when the sun was in Taurus on March 21, 3000 BC, at the vernal equinox.

Chapter 7

The Planets in St. Peter's Basilica

Fig. 7-1. St. Helen and the symbol of Saturn.

Now we return to those sculptures at floor level in St. Peter's displayed in the huge supports of the transept arches. This figure is St. Helen, the mother of Constantine. She is not mentioned in the Bible. What is she doing there? Isn't this a Christian church even though it is Catholic? Who gave them the right to put a woman not even mentioned in the story of Jesus into his holy church?

Helen was a Christian, and she traveled to Jerusalem in the late third century. She went to the tomb of Jesus and supposedly found a piece of the true cross there. She collected it and took it back to Rome, where it is seen rarely these days as a relic of the church. Her symbol is of the true cross of which she discovered. A common joke amongst historians is that enough wood was found from the true cross to be able to build six houses.

I want to point out that the shape of Helen is very similar to the ancient symbol of Saturn. This symbol goes back at least one thousand years, so it was created before the new St. Peter's was ever planned. Compare the ancient symbol of Saturn with the shape of the sculpture, and draw your own conclusion. They appear to be very similar.

The ancient symbol of Mars

Mars painting from Pompey, 100 BC?

Fig. 7-2. Longinus

Fig. 7-3 Mars

Are there any similarities between the 100 BC Mars (Fig. 7-3) and the AD 1590 Longinus? St. Longinus is very similar to Mars

The next sculpture to look at is Longinus, the soldier who pierced Jesus's side. Water is the symbol of Pisces the Fish, the zodiacal symbol on the crucifixion of Christ. We see Longinus with a spear or lance. Now look at the ancient painting of Mars from Pompey on the right from 100 BC. It shows the god of war with a spear, a shield, and some armor. Compare the pedestals. How similar they do appear?

Fig. 7-5B Venus symbol

Fig. 7-4. St. Veronica

Fig. 7-5 Aphrodite

St. Veronica of AD 1570 is similar to Fig. 7-5, Botticelli's AD 1458 Venus.

Next, we shall take a look at St. Veronica. Her story is also not mentioned in the Bible. She supposedly took a veil, put it over Jesus's face, and came away with a perfect icon of his. The name Veronica literally means "perfect icon" in Latin. This sculpture received a lot of criticism over the centuries for the very provocative view of her legs and thighs. She looks rather sexy. That is precisely the way the ancients saw Venus. She was looked at as a sexy lady known as Aphrodite or Venus. Compare the painting by Botticelli from 1458 and the Veronica sculpture, and see the similarity. Isaiah 14:12 mentions Lucifer as the day star. The Latin word Lucifer means "phosphorus" or "Venus."

Look below St. Veronica on the pedestal, and see a seashell symbol. It is curious that Botticelli's 1458 painting of Venus has her riding on a seashell. One explanation is that this is a symbol of the Catholic financial patron for these sculptures.

Fig. 7-6.

Jupiter from the buried city of Pompeii AD 40.

St. Andrew and Jupiter

♃

Fig. 7-7. The St. Andrew

This sculpture is similar to the ancient symbol of Jupiter (Jovis). St. Andrew is one of the twelve disciples of Jesus. He was crucified sideways on a cross. Here we see the sculpture of St. Andrew in this portico. Now look at the symbol of Jupiter, shown on the right. It looks like a sideways cross. Also look at the small painting of Jupiter on his throne from Pompey in the upper right. That must have been painted previous to the AD 70 eruption that obliterated the city. Once again, the symbol of Jupiter looks similar to the sculpture. Is it merely a coincidence that all four of the sculptures bear such striking resemblances to the ancient symbols of the major planets?

Fig. 7-8. These are not Biblical

Only one out the three main sculptures in St. Peter's is known to be biblical, the mention of Andrew as one of the disciples of Christ. The other names, Veronica, Helen, and Longinus, are not mentioned in the Bible.

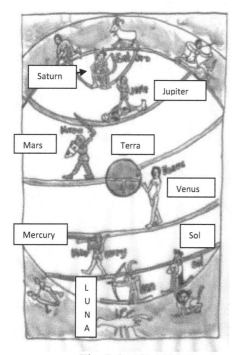

The known universe from AD 1400. The Earth was thought to be at the center. The planets were considered to be gods. The gods, the sun, and the moon orbited around Earth. It appears as if they even thought the moon (luna) and sun (sol) were floating on a boat. Notice the zodiacal figures are the same as we know them today.

Fig. 7-9. AD 1400 Cosmos

Here we see a rendition from the fifteenth century. It shows in the middle, Earth, as a T for terra. Above Earth is Mars with his sword. Above Mars is Jupiter. The figure lying down is unknown, but for some reason, Jupiter is shown with this dead-looking figure. Above Jupiter, we see Saturn with a scythe, as he is the god of the end of harvest. Below T is Venus, the goddess of love and beauty. Below Venus is Mercury with his winged cap and bugle announcement like the cock crowing. Below Mercury is the moon on the left and the sun on the right. These seven celestial gods are what the seven days of the week are named after: Sunday (the sun), Monday (the moon), Tuesday (Mars), Wednesday (Mercury), Thursday (Jupiter), Friday (Venus), and Saturday (Saturn).

Galileo's
moon

Fig. 7-10. Mary standing on top of Galileo's moon sketch that he made in 1609.

      Mary is on St. Peter's dome. While the Bible does not say Mary is like the moon, she was often associated with Diana or Artemis as a goddess of the moon. "A woman clothed with the sun, with the moon under her feet and on her head a crown of twelve stars" (Rev. 12:1). This is often referred to as Mary. In the above painting, we see Mary standing on top of the moon with twelve stars above her. Cigoli, an Italian painter and close friend of Galileo, painted it in 1610. Cigoli painted a copy of Galileo's moon sketch, which was published in 1609. He painted this one year after Galileo published his "Starry Messenger" sketch of the moon. In both Isaiah 13:10 and Ezekiel 32:7, it mentions curious passages that give us clues to the moon being feminine. Isaiah 13:10 (KJV) reads, "The sun shall be darkened in *his* going forth, and the moon shall not cause *her* light to shine." The important aspect is it says "her." There is also a reference in Jeremiah 7:18, "the queen of heaven." This is often associated with the goddesses Astarte, Virgo, or Persephone.

Fig. 7-11. Paul (Mercury) and Mary (the Moon) on the dome

Now I have shown you the amazing similarity between the four saints and the four brightest planets, Venus, Mars, Jupiter, and Saturn. Where is Mercury and the moon? Both are up on the dome of St. Peter's. On the right side, we see the figures of St. Paul and Mary. The Bible said Paul was likened to Hermes (Mercury) in Acts 14:11, and Mary was often depicted with the moon (Fig. 7-10). Notice the curious-looking "half-moon" shape to Mary's lower left.

Ezekiel 32:7 states, "The moon shall not give *her* light." This is also repeated in Matthew 24:29 and Mark 13:24 as "the sun will be darkened and the moon shall not give off its own light."

It was and is a lack of understanding science to say that the moon gives off light. Science can confirm that moonlight is reflecting sunlight and the moon does not give off its own light, like the sun does.

Chapter 8

The Layout of St. Peter's Is Geocentric

Fig. 8-1.St. Peter's Chair

We are now looking at the great Bernini (sun) window and the Chair of St. Peter, a gift of Charles the Bald in AD 875. St. Peter could not possibly have sat on it. He had been dead for eight hundred years. Many gold saint-like figures are nearby, and there are some angels, as St. Peter was the first pope. I call this window the "sun window." It looks so much like a sunset with the rays of the sun jutting outward. The sun window is in the western apse of the basilica. At sunset, it really lights up, especially around Easter. Notice the gold embellishment all around it. Reminds one of the sun, doesn't it? If we were to step back a few feet, we would see the spiraled baldachin pillars. They are eccentric spiral shapes. Pope Barberini had the bronze roof of the Pantheon removed and melted down in 1580 and then cast into these columns. "What the barbarians could not do Barberini did in just a few years." [19]They are referring to his scuttling of resources to build St. Peter's. Now, look at the upper left, and see the blue W that signifies Matthew. Then look to the right and see the orange F of John. The pendentives of Matthew and John are located right above them. Make a mental note of the position of the sun window and St. Peter's chair in relationship to the W and F.

---

[19] J.H.Douglas, The Principal Noble Families of Rome, Rome 1905
www/crystalinks.com/romepantheon.html

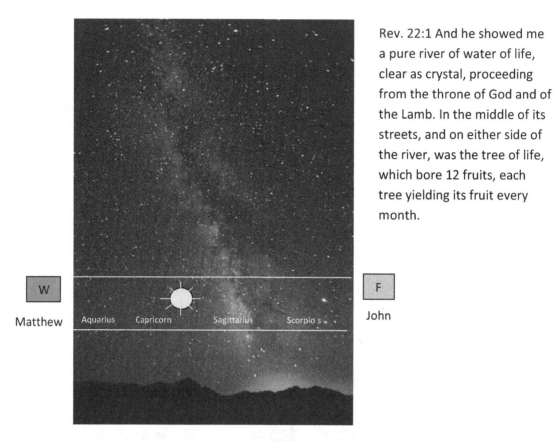

Rev. 22:1 And he showed me a pure river of water of life, clear as crystal, proceeding from the throne of God and of the Lamb. In the middle of its streets, and on either side of the river, was the tree of life, which bore 12 fruits, each tree yielding its fruit every month.

Fig. 8-2. The zodiac crossing the Milky Way.

The sun window is in between the blue W on the left and the orange F on the right. Now, look at the above image. See the sun as a yellow symbol located in between the blue W and the orange F. The sun is just to the left of Sagittarius, the center area of the Milky Way. This was the location of the sun on December 21, AD 0. The blue W of Matthew is located in Aquarius to the left, and the orange F of John is located to the right and in Scorpios. The Revelation 22:1 passage sounds like a great description of this part of the night sky. "And he showed me a pure river of water of life, clear as crystal, proceeding from the throne of God and of the Lamb. In the middle of its streets, and on either side of the river, was the tree of life, which bore twelve fruits, each tree yielding its fruits every month." The pure river is like the Milky Way. The twelve fruits are like the twelve zodiacal signs of every month intersecting the "river" of the Milky Way twice a year.

We next see a floor plan view of St. Peter's. Look at the center, and see a dark blue dot representing Earth. This is where the baldachin is located. Recall that it has four pillars, a flat roof, corners, and edges, a perfect depiction of how Earth is described in the Bible. Above, up on the dome is the Mary figure (a small white dot), likened to the moon, and the Paul figure, likened to Mercury. Then we see the surrounding four colored dots representing the major planets. The yellow dot is Veronica (Venus). The large orange with red stripe dot is Andrew (Jupiter), the red is Longinus (Mars), and the gray is Helen (Saturn).

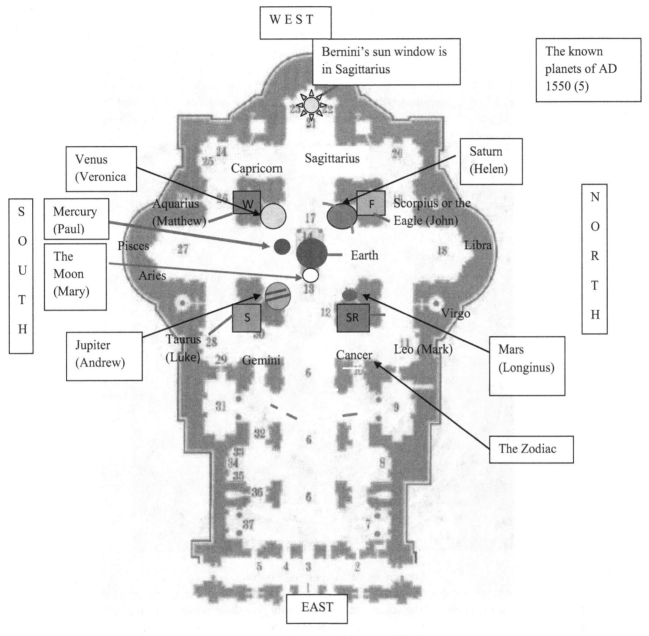

Bernini's sun window is in Sagittarius

The known planets of AD 1550 (5)

Venus (Veronica

Saturn (Helen)

Capricorn

Sagittarius

SOUTH

Mercury (Paul)

Aquarius (Matthew)

W

F

Scorpius or the Eagle (John)

NORTH

The Moon (Mary)

Pisces

Earth

Libra

Aries

Jupiter (Andrew)

Taurus (Luke)

S

SR

Virgo

Mars (Longinus)

Gemini

Cancer

Leo (Mark)

The Zodiac

EAST

Fig 8-3. The Earth centered layout of St. Peter's

The four Gospel writers are the four royal Persian stars of the zodiac. Look at the upper left for the blue W representing Matthew/Aquarius. Below that on the left side is the light-green S representing Luke/Taurus. To the right is the dark-green SR representing Mark/Leo. Above Mark (SR) is the orange F representing John /the Eagle/fall. So we have a zodiacal layout that is in the proper order. Start with the light-blue W in Aquarius. Move to the left, and see Pisces. Below that is Aries. Then move counterclockwise to Taurus, Gemini, Cancer, Leo, Virgo, Libra, Scorpio, Sagittarius, and Capricorn. The four royal Persian stars in St. Peter's are in the correct order. Now look at the top and see the big sun dot representing Bernini's sun window. Here we see the sun is in Sagittarius and slightly near to Capricorn. That is where the sun was located at the time of Christ's birth on Christmas Day. Notice the opposite direction faces east, and the sun was in Gemini on June 21, the summer solstice. Thus, St. Peter's is laid out like a sun's annual movement indicator. The long axis faces east-west and Sagittarius-Gemini. The short axis of the cross faces north-south and Pisces-Virgo. This is where the sun was located on the spring equinox (March 21) and the autumnal equinox (September 21). Therefore, on March 21 (around Easter), the noontime sun will shine directly into the south-facing window, number twenty-seven.

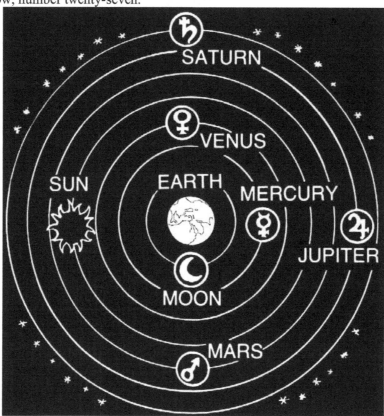

Fig. 8-4. Archaic Earth centered layout

This sixteenth-century model of the known solar system is incorrect. Science confirms that the sun is in the center of the solar system, not Earth. Are there similarities to the layout of this geocentric plan and St. Peter's? Here, we see the incorrect model of Earth in the center and the moon nearby. Then there's Mercury, Venus, and the sun orbiting Earth, along with Mars, Jupiter, and Saturn. For fifteen hundred years, it was believed that this Earth-centered solar system was an accurate layout of the universe. The church accepted it. St. Peter's is laid out in much the same pattern as this. Earth was thought to be motionless, and the sun was thought to orbit around it. Copernicus disproved this in 1543. He waited until his deathbed to reveal *De Revolutions* because he feared the Catholic Church burning him alive. His book radically announced a sun-centered solar system. Could this be the real reason Galileo's sun-centered proposal got him in so much trouble with the Catholic Church? Was it because he threw doubt into the layout of the new St. Peter's Earth-centered floor plan with his sun-centered affirmation? Was that heresy why he was sentenced to house arrest for the rest of his life?

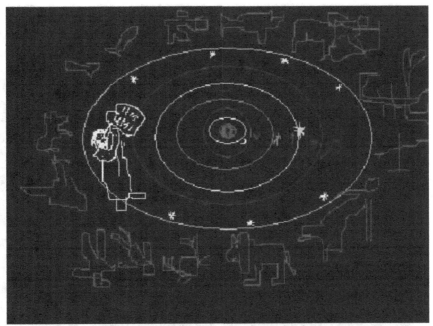

Fig. 8-5. Wrong Earth centered solar system

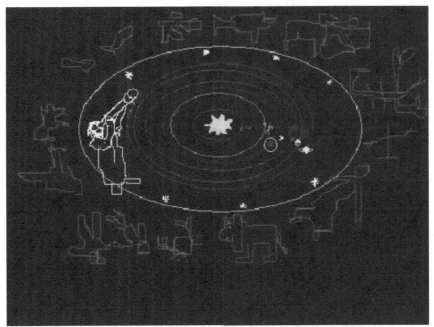

Fig. 8-6. Correct sun centered solar system

The incorrect geocentric model is on top, (Fig. 8-5) and the correct heliocentric model of the solar system is on the bottom.(Fig. 8-6) Notice the Earth-centered solar system (top) has a man holding up scriptures to the heavens while the sun-centered solar system (bottom) has him looking through a telescope.

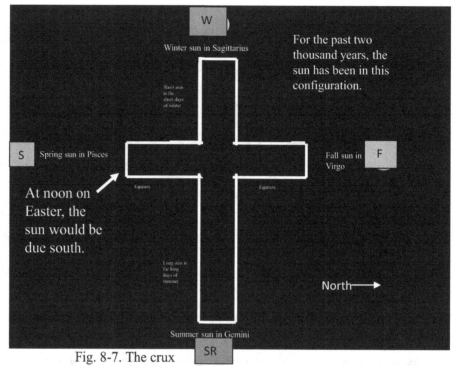

Fig. 8-7. The crux

The drawing above shows the crux-shaped layout of St. Peter's. The Basilica is laid out with each axis pointing to where the sun was located at the four seasons of the year two thousand years ago, or at the time of Christ's birth. Starting at the top and moving counterclockwise, we see the blue W is in Sagittarius, the light-green S is in Pisces, the dark-green SR is in Gemini, and the orange F is in Virgo. The astrological layout of St. Peter's (based on the location where the four pendentives are) will expire two hundred years from now when the sun moves into Aquarius.

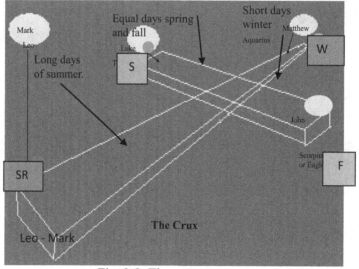

Fig. 8-8. The crux.

The preceding page shows the position of the sun five thousand years ago when the sun was in Taurus the Bull on the first day of spring March 21, 3000 BC. Today, it is in Pisces. In those days, the sun was in Aquarius in the winter solstice, in Leo in the summer solstice, and in Scorpio/the Eagle in the fall. This is not how St. Peter's is laid out. It has the sun in Pisces at noon at spring. They laid the zodiacal pattern out to where the sun was in the year 0. Also notice the crux is made up of a long and short axis. The long axis has the short section on top, which illustrates the short days of winter, and the long axis on the bottom, which illustrates the long days of summer. It also shows us the equal transept, which illustrates the equal days of spring and fall. The crux is simply an allegorical tool to illustrate the sun's annual four seasons.

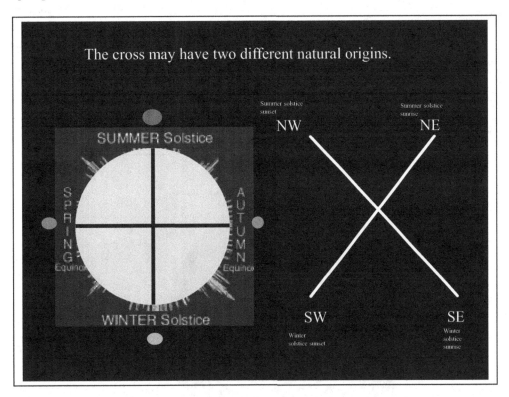

Fig. 8-9. Variations of crux shapes

The crux can have other depictions. On the left is the Celtic idea of the four positions of the sun during the year. It incorporates a circle into the design. The drawing on the right is more like Stonehenge. The sun rises in the northeast on June 21 and sets in the southwest on December 21. The sun rises in the southeast on December 21 and sets in the northwest on June 21. From plotting these sunrise/sunset positions, we can create a crux pattern.

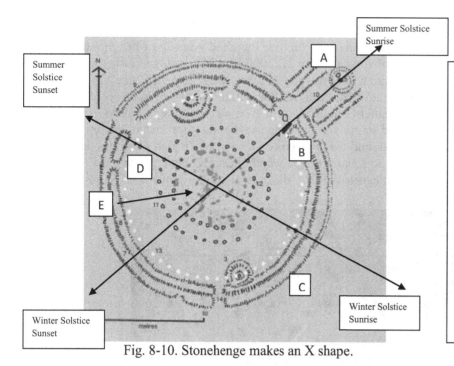

This overhead view of Stonehenge shows the location of the heel stone (A) on the upper right side. It aligns with another stone (B) on the summer solstice and centers on the altar (E). Two other stones seem to align with the winter solstice sunrise at (C) and the other stone at (D). This makes an X shape, the crux. These four positions would also be where the four royal Persian stars are located.

Fig. 8-10. Stonehenge makes an X shape.

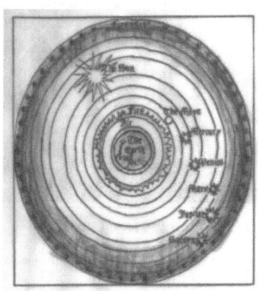

Fig. 8-11. This sketch from around the year 1380 demonstrates the belief in a geocentric model of the cosmos. They followed the idea of Ptolemy that Earth was at the center and everything orbited it. This model was accepted until well after the death of Copernicus in 1543 and after Galileo passed away in 1642 and his book, *The Dialogue*, had been published. The Catholic Church did not approve his book until 1820 when they lifted the ban on his writings. It wasn't until 1992 that the Church acknowledged they had done wrongs to Galileo and asked for forgiveness. It took four hundred years, but Galileo's sun-centered theory was finally accepted.

Biblical views of the Earth

1. The four corners of the Earth. Ezek. 7:2 and Rev. 7:1

2. Ends of the Earth. Ps. 59:13 and 61:2, Isa. 41:9, Jer. 51:16

3. Pillars of the Earth. 1 Sam. 2:8 and Job 9:6

A flat Earth with edges and corners frightened the early transocean explorers.

See photo below.

4. World stands firm never to be moved. 1 Chr. 16:30 and Ps. 93:1

5. The devil took Jesus up to the highest mountain and showed him all of the kingdoms of the Earth. Matt. 4:8

Fig. 8-12 The Bible and a Flat Earth.

Fig. 8-13 The edge of the Earth

The Bible does not demonstrate nor explain Earth as a sphere nor a ball. It does say that, from a high point, Earth is likened to a circle, but this is a ring, a one-dimensional circle that we call the horizon. The Bible gives us several clues regarding how the ancients regarded Earth. It says it has four corners, ends, and pillars. It says it stands firm and, from a high mountain, all kingdoms can be seen. That would be a flat world. You cannot see more than twenty miles with a curved Earth, as it drops below the horizon. It is no wonder that Magellan feared he would fall off the edge of the world.

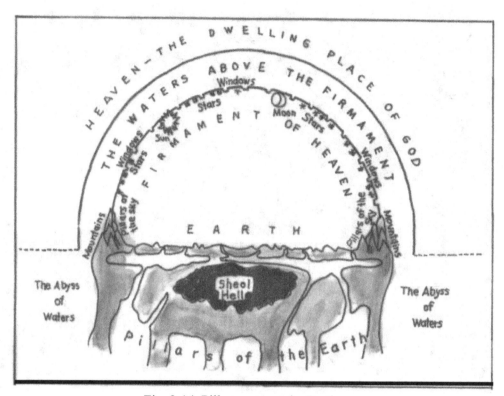

Fig. 8-14. Pillars support the Earth

The Bible authors thought pillars supported Earth (1 Sam. 2:8). Hell was deep down in the bowels of Earth (Sheol) (Deut. 32:22). Earth was flat (Matt. 4:8). There were more pillars holding up the dome of the sky or the firmament of heaven (Job 26:11). Waters were above that, and the highest point was the realm of God. Heaven was the dwelling place of God at the perimeter. This is exactly how the baldachins in St. Peter's are laid out.

The Astronomy of Genesis Lacks Scientific Accuracy

The book of Genesis 1 begins by saying, "In the beginning, God created the heavens and the earth." Let's imagine that scene. First God creates the heavens. So what are they? Let's imagine some kind of big, open void. Where was God when he created it? Was he outside of the heavens? What dimensions would he give to the heavens? What was the composition of the heavens? Next, God creates the Earth and places it inside of that void. Now, it could be interpreted that he might have created the two (the heavens and the Earth) simultaneously. The Bible says God moved over the waters. Then in 1:3, he adds some light for day and darkness for night. He then somehow brings on morning (remembering that the Earth's rotation causes morning), and this is one twenty-four-hour day. That is the end of Day One. So we have a waterish void in which is placed the Earth. **This is a geocentric Earth idea.** There is nothing else at this beginning except the Earth and the heavens. It is not until Day Four that God creates the stars, the sun, and the moon. We know this is not the scientifically accurate way things occurred. **The sun must have been created before the Earth.**

*Read more in *Universe* by Kaufmann Freedman Press

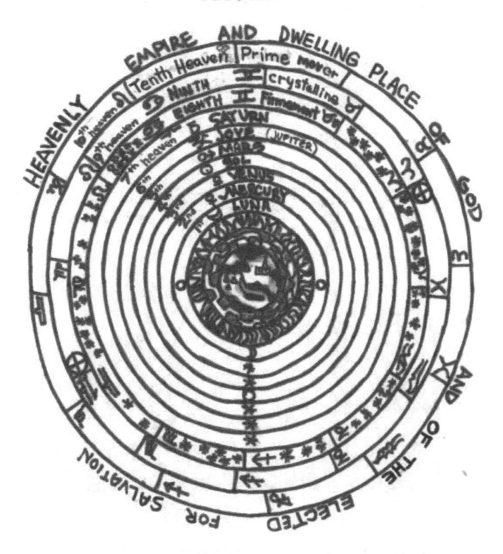

Fig. 8-15. An archaic AD 1539 view of the cosmos.

Once again, the Aristotelian and Ptolemaic universe held that Earth was in the center, followed by the many spheres of the planets and the sun, then the zodiac and the stars, and finally the "heavenly empire and dwelling place of God." Jerusalem and a church are generally shown as being at the center of Earth. The "heavenly empire," which is translated from "*coelum empireum*," is probably where they thought Earth's heat came from. We now know that Earth's heat comes from the sun.

Fig. 8-16. The Earth-centered Baldachin.

Now let's look at the baldachin constructed over the tomb of St. Peter's. It has four pillars supporting a flat roof with edges and corners. There are the planets surrounding it, the Bernini sun window, the zodiacal symbols, and the dome of heaven up above. It is set up identical to the Aristotelian viewpoint of the universe. St. Peter's dome has sixteen figures on it, including the eleven disciples. (Judas is not up there; John the Baptist is in his place at twelfth). There is Jesus (thirteenth), St. Paul (fourteenth), Longinus (fifteenth), and Mary (sixteenth). At the highest, we see some stars, and in the very center is the realm of God. This is much the same as the ancient model of the cosmos with Earth in the center and God looking down upon us from up above.

Fig.8-17. God at the top of St. Peter's

Way up in the middle of St. Peter's dome is God on the highest. He is reaching down to everyone with an open hand as if he is going to touch him or her. This is the very highest peak of the dome in St. Peter's. Here we see some stars on the farthest periphery, eight angels, and God himself looking down to everyone with an outstretched arm. We notice that God looks like the Old Testament God. He is an elderly man. He is a Caucasian man with a white beard. He is not unlike Santa Claus in appearance. This viewpoint tells us something about the cosmology of this church. Did they take into consideration that the majority of the population on Planet Earth is not Caucasian? One can only wonder if they had questioned the races of the world, say those people living in the Amazon, Australia, Central Africa, or China. Would those races approve of this viewpoint of the Almighty? With seven billion people on Earth and more than five billion of the world's people being non-Caucasian, then one might wonder why those five billion don't ask themselves, "Why God wouldn't look more like us? We are the majority."[20]

One additional thought comes to mind. Why wasn't Jesus shown at the highest point? Doesn't the church praise Jesus as Hosanna or Emmanuel, the Lord of Lords, King of Kings? Why not show the Trinity? Why not show St. Peter looking down with his keys in hand? The inscription around the medallion reads "Glorious St. Peter and Pope Sixtus in 1587."

---

[20] www.worldometers.info/world-population

www.city-data.com/forum/politics-other-controversies/1719342-how-many-white-people-do-you.html

Fig. 8-18. Pope John Paul II.   Fig. 8-19. Pope Benedict.

Fig. 8-20. A monstrance.   Fig. 8-21. An ostensorium.

The association with sun worship continues to this day in the Catholic Church. Here we see the monstrance or the ostensorium being held by John Paul II on the left and Pope Benedict on the right. It is the most venerated symbol to be displayed within the church. It appears obvious that it is a symbol of the sun. See the disc shape and the rays of the sun. Where else does it come from? It is ancient sun worship incorporated into the church.

Chapter 9

The Many Versions of the Zodiac in the Church

Fig. 9-1. Arles Notre Dame Portico.

On this portico of Arles Notre Dame Church in France, see the four cherubs surrounding the central figure of Jesus. The cherubs have wings and can be identified with the four royal Persian stars. The figure on the lower left near the dark-green SR is Mark/Leo. The figure near the blue W is Matthew/Aquarius. Near the orange F is John/Eagle, and near the light-green S is Luke/Taurus. They are arranged in a counterclockwise circle, starting with Luke/Taurus being spring, up to John/Eagle as fall, across to Matthew/Aquarius as winter, and down to Mark/Leo as summer. The twelve disciples are below him.

Fig. 9-2. Val de Grace pendentives of the four Gospel writers inside of the great cathedral in Paris, France. On the upper left near the blue W is Matthew with the little man representing Aquarius. On the lower left is the light-green S with Luke and the bull's head to the right of him. On the lower right near the orange F is John and the Eagle. Upper right shows Mark at SR with a lion's head slightly to his right and representing Leo the Lion.

Fig. 9-3. The dome of Val de Grace and the four symbols.

Hagia Sophia was a church and then a mosque. Now, it's a museum in Istanbul (Constantinople), Turkey.

Fig. 9-4. The author in front of Hagia Sophia in Istanbul, Turkey.

It was a Christian church that Constantine originally built in 360, but it was rebuilt a couple times since. In 1453, Sultan Mehmed II conquered the city of Constantinople, and he ordered the church to be converted into a mosque. In 1935, it became a museum. More interior views are seen in Fig. 9-5 and 6.

Fig. 9-5.   Fig. 9-6.

Fig. 9-7. The ceiling of Hagia Sophia.

      This is the interior of Hagia Sophia. See the Arabic writing in the middle. Notice in each of the four corners, there are some feathery-looking beings mentioned in Isaiah 6:2 as six-winged seraphim that are painted onto the transept supports below the dome. The dome at one time had a magnificent painting of Christ, but it was painted over.

      This is a perfect representation of the masking effect of religion. An old religion can be painted over the old and then called something new, yet it there is still the old religion underneath.

Fig. 9-8. The face of cherubim on Hagia Sophia (Photo by Nitin Bhardwaj).

Art restorers looking under a medallion of one of the cherubim in Hagia Sophia only recently discovered this face in 2009. It is most likely one of the four Gospel writers. John was usually depicted as the younger looking of the four. Who knows? In coming years, they might be able to see the other three faces.

Here is the Christ image on one of the walls in Hagi Sophia. Notice the halo behind his head and the four directions. They are symbolic of the sun's corona and the four seasons.

Fig. 9-9. Christ on Hagia Sophia.

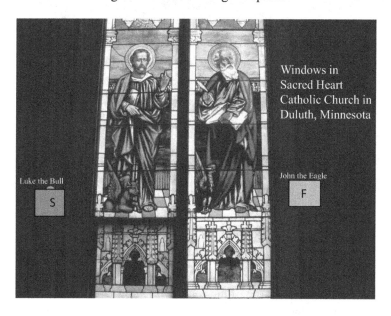

Fig. 9-10. St.Luke and St. John in Sacred Heart

In the author's local area, there are several churches with the four evangelists/royal Persian stars upon them. This is the stained glass window inside of Sacred Heart Catholic Church in Duluth, Minnesota. On the left, we see Luke with the ox or bull by his feet. On the right is John with the eagle.

Fig. 9-11. The lion and the man in Sacred Heart Church.

Here we see St. Mark on the left with the lion figure. On the right is St. Matthew with the man.

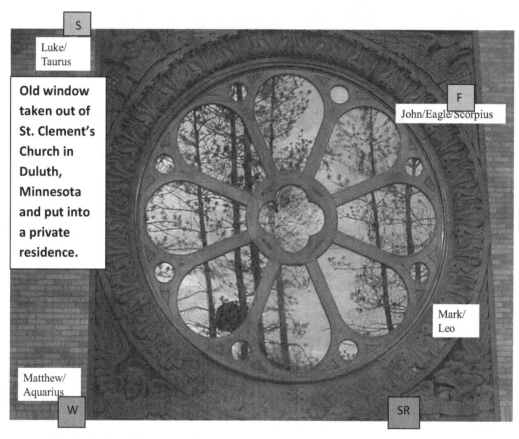

Fig. 9-12. St. Clement's church window showing the four royal symbols.

Here is the window from St. Clement's Church in Duluth, Minnesota. It was made in the early twentieth century and is now on the façade of a private residence in Normanna Township. On the upper left, you can see the light-green S of the ox of St. Luke. On the lower left is the winged man with St. Matthew and the blue W. On the lower right is the dark-green SR near the winged lion with St. Mark. The upper right corner shows an orange F near the eagle with St. John. St. Luke is spring. Then go diagonally across to St. Mark and summer. Move up to St. John/fall and diagonally across to St. Matthew/winter and up to spring. Going from season to season, it will lay out a huge X.

Fig. 9-13. Holy Rosary façade.

This is the façade of Holy Rosary Church in Duluth, Minnesota. See the four creatures in the tiles. The lower left is spring, the lower right is summer, the upper right is fall, and winter is the upper left. It is laid out the same as St. Peter's. This zodiacal pattern flows counterclockwise from Luke/spring to Mark/summer, up to John/fall, over to Matthew/winter, and then full circle to spring.

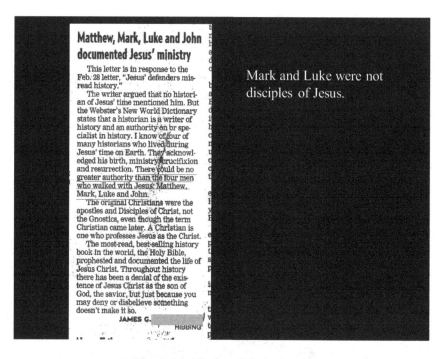

Fig. 9-14. Mark and Luke

Many people believe Matthew, Mark, Luke, and John were walking with Jesus. However, Mark and Luke were companions of Paul, not disciples of Jesus.

Mark and Luke were not the names of Jesus's disciples. So why were they so important? They were companions of Paul, whose name was Saul (Sol) and changed to Paul (Pol) (Apollo.)

The names of the twelve disciples are Peter, Andrew, James, John, Philip, Bartholomew, Thomas, Matthew, James, Thaddaeus, Simon, and Judas.

Matthew 10

Fig. 9-15. Sol changed to Pol

More solar mystery is attached to the New Testament story as Saul's name is changed to Paul in Acts 13:9. Another way to read it is Sol becomes Pol. Sol is the sun, and Pol is Apollo, the sun god.[1] Jesus had twelve disciples. The sun moves through twelve signs of the zodiac. More sun allegory is entrenched into the story.

---

[1] S. Acharya, *The Christ Conspiracy*, 173.

Fig. 9-16. European church doors.   Fig. 9-17. Irish church tapestry.

All throughout Europe, one can see the four Gospel writers/zodiacal signs on medieval church doors and tapestries. The door on the left is a large door with St. Matthew/Aquarius in the upper right, St. Mark/Leo the Lion on the upper left, St. John/Eagle on the lower left, and St. Luke/Taurus the Bull on the lower right. Notice the white horse in the middle with a halo and a cross. The tapestry on the right is from the *Book of Kells*, dated to around AD 800, and comes from Ireland and again shows the four royal Persian stars.

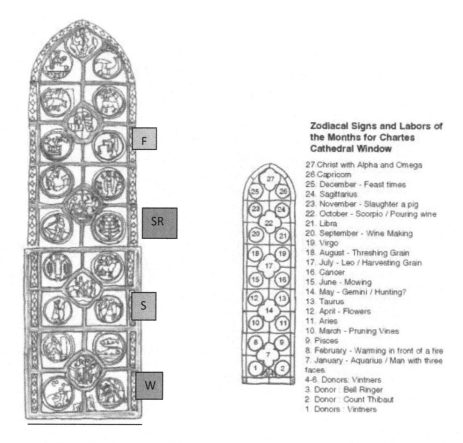

Zodiacal Signs and Labors of the Months for Chartes Cathedral Window

27. Christ with Alpha and Omega
26. Capricorn
25. December - Feast times
24. Sagittarius
23. November - Slaughter a pig
22. October - Scorpio / Pouring wine
21. Libra
20. September - Wine Making
19. Virgo
18. August - Threshing Grain
17. July - Leo / Harvesting Grain
16. Cancer
15. June - Mowing
14. May - Gemini / Hunting?
13. Taurus
12. April - Flowers
11. Aries
10. March - Pruning Vines
9. Pisces
8. February - Warming in front of a fire
7. January - Aquarius / Man with three faces
4-6. Donors: Vintners
3. Donor : Bell Ringer
2. Donor : Count Thibaut
1. Donors : Vintners

| Fig. 9-18. Chartres window. | Fig. 9-19. Chartres window designation. |

The great cathedral of Chartres in France has the zodiac displayed on a large front window. At the top is displayed Christ. Below him is Scorpio at F and then Leo at SR. Then curiously enough, Gemini is at S. This is an error on the part of the window designer. It should have been Taurus. Putting Gemini in this position puts it out of sequence with the five thousand-year-ago configuration of the royal Persian stars. W is at Aquarius. Intertwined with the signs of the zodiac are the twelve labors. Below is another incorporation of the four royal Persian stars into the Vatican. See the bull with Luke?

Fig. 9-20. The Sala Dei Palafrenieri.

Within the Vatican compound, there is the private sanctuary for the pope, the Sala Dei Palafrenieri, or the room of the grooms. One can call it the pope's inner sanctuary. The large painting of St. Luke/Taurus the Bull is to the left of the private entrance. Taurus was where the sun was located in 3000 BC and could be deemed a portal to the new year at that time. It was the Age of the Bull. Notice the four royal Persian stars from left to right of the Eagle, Scorpio (F), the Lion/Leo (SR), the Bull of Taurus (S), and the Man/Aquarius (W). Raphael painted them in 1511.

Fig. 9-21. The Sala Dei Palafrenieri with the four cardinal symbols.

Once again, see the doorway to the pope's inner sanctuary near the light-green S. That signifies Taurus. To the left is the dark-green SR (Leo) and then the orange F (Eagle). One might wonder what the four signs of the zodiac have to do with the pope's prayers, but further significance of them as the Gospel writers is understandable.

Chapter 10

The Zodiacal Timeline from Bulls to Lamb to Fish

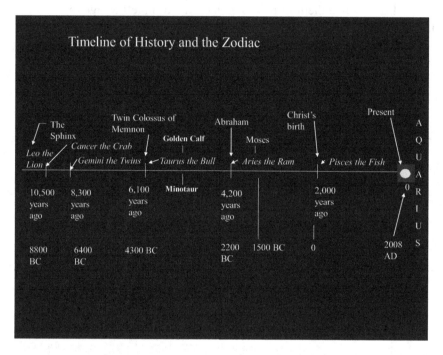

Fig. 10-1. A timeline history of religion and where the sun is in the zodiac.

In this timeline, we can see the present era on the far right at the 0 point. Moving to the left, we can see two thousand years of Pisces the Fish. This is the era of the sun being in Pisces since the time of Christ's birth. Then from AD 0 back until 2200 BC was the era of when the sun was in Aries the Ram. This is the era of the Lamb of God. All kinds of lamb/ram worship were going on in the Mediterranean. Osiris was the shepherd, and Amon-Ra was a kind of ram god. Moses has the blood of a lamb spread on the doorpost and lintels. He also had destroyed the golden calf, a symbol that the Age of the Bull was behind them. Jesus was deemed the Lamb of God. It is always bulls, rams, lambs, and fish, and they have something to do with the signs of the zodiac. Why not pandas or kangaroos?

From 2200 BC to 4300 BC is the time when the sun was in Taurus the Bull. That is when all kinds of bull worship sprang up like the Minotaur, Cretan Bulls, and Apis bull (the sacred cows of India). Mithra slays the Bull of Heaven. Moses symbolically smashes the golden calf.

From 4300 BC to 6400 BC, the sun was in Gemini on March 21. Perhaps this was the era of the Twin Colossus of Memnon. Previous to 8800 BC, the sun was in Leo the Lion. And who knows? The Sphinx may be a memory of that golden era.

Fig. 10-2. The sun enters Aries (2000 BC) (Stellarium).

Around 2000 BC, the sun moved into Aries, the lamb/ram on the vernal equinox. This would be the era of the lamb/ram symbology.

Fig. 10-3. Ram/lamb worship in Egypt.

Here are some of the 1000 BC temples dedicated to Amon-Ra at Karnak in Egypt. Ram worship sprung up all throughout the Mediterranean region around this time. Why? Could it be that the sun was in the sign of Aries the Ram during this era?

Fig. 10-4. Moses in *The Ten Commandments* and the blood of the lamb

Moses had the blood of the lamb spread along the doorposts and lintels to allow God to pass over and spare the Hebrews. The Egyptians' fate was far more severe as God killed the firstborn sons.

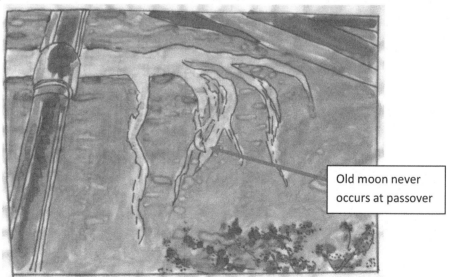

Old moon never occurs at passover

Fig. 10-5. God's wrath

In *The Ten Commandments*, watch this scene as God's retribution to the nonconfiding Egyptians was to send down a sinister finger-looking menace. Because Passover occurs only at the first full moon after the spring equinox, you can see this old crescent moon is an inaccuracy in the movie.

Fig. 10-6. The Lamb

This is a photo of the Lamb of God as seen in Holy Rosary Catholic church in Duluth, Minnesota. It shows the sun halo and crux-like form behind the head and upon the flag. All are symbols of the sun's annual journey. Could the four stars be the four royal Persian stars? The seven candlesticks are mentioned in Revelation and may relate to the Seven Sisters, the stars of the Pleiades.

The ram or Lamb of God symbols had to do with the sun being in Aries.

Fig. 10-7. The shepherd

For thousands of years before Christ, the Egyptians considered Osiris the true shepherd. His symbol was the shepherd's crook. The era of the lamb had barely come to an end when Jesus became associated with the shepherd. It all had to do with the sun's position along the zodiac.

Chapter 11

The Twelve Signs of the Zodiac

Fig. 11-1. Mithra killing the Bull

In this rendition above of a relief from AD 100, we see Mithra killing the Bull of Heaven, symbolizing the sun in Taurus the Bull on the vernal equinox five thousand years ago. The twelve signs of the zodiac surround Mithra, a kind of sun god.

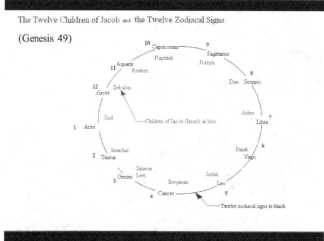

Fig. 11-2 The twelve

Now we shall investigate the association of the twelve zodiacal constellations incorporated into religion. The twelve children of Jacob can be demonstrated as nearly the same as the twelve zodiacal signs.

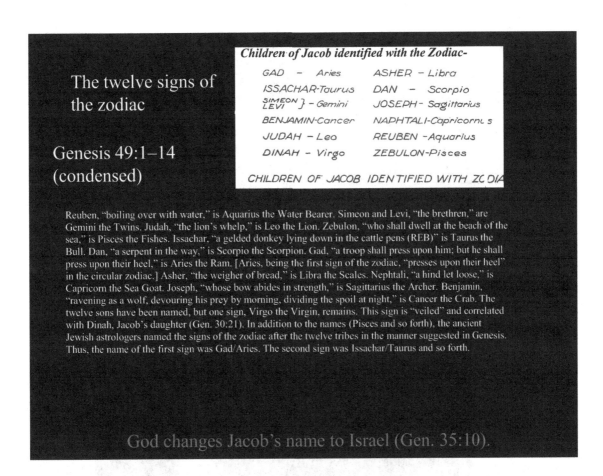

The twelve signs of the zodiac

Genesis 49:1–14 (condensed)

Children of Jacob identified with the Zodiac-

GAD – Aries	ASHER – Libra
ISSACHAR-Taurus	DAN – Scorpio
SIMEON LEVI } – Gemini	JOSEPH – Sagittarius
BENJAMIN-Cancer	NAPHTALI-Capricornus
JUDAH – Leo	REUBEN –Aquarius
DINAH – Virgo	ZEBULON-Pisces

CHILDREN OF JACOB IDENTIFIED WITH ZODIA

Reuben, "boiling over with water," is Aquarius the Water Bearer. Simeon and Levi, "the brethren," are Gemini the Twins. Judah, "the lion's whelp," is Leo the Lion. Zebulon, "who shall dwell at the beach of the sea," is Pisces the Fishes. Issachar, "a gelded donkey lying down in the cattle pens (REB)" is Taurus the Bull. Dan, "a serpent in the way," is Scorpio the Scorpion. Gad, "a troop shall press upon him; but he shall press upon their heel," is Aries the Ram. [Aries, being the first sign of the zodiac, "presses upon their heel" in the circular zodiac.] Asher, "the weigher of bread," is Libra the Scales. Nephtali, "a hind let loose," is Capricorn the Sea Goat. Joseph, "whose bow abides in strength," is Sagittarius the Archer. Benjamin, "ravening as a wolf, devouring his prey by morning, dividing the spoil at night," is Cancer the Crab. The twelve sons have been named, but one sign, Virgo the Virgin, remains. This sign is "veiled" and correlated with Dinah, Jacob's daughter (Gen. 30:21). In addition to the names (Pisces and so forth), the ancient Jewish astrologers named the signs of the zodiac after the twelve tribes in the manner suggested in Genesis. Thus, the name of the first sign was Gad/Aries. The second sign was Issachar/Taurus and so forth.

God changes Jacob's name to Israel (Gen. 35:10).

Fig. 11-3. The children of Jacob and the zodiac.

During the year, the sun appears to move through all twelve signs of the zodiac along its annual journey. The story of Jacob and his children can readily be demonstrated as an allegory of that same story. You can read in the white box above the names of the children of Jacob and then the Genesis 49:1–14 version of each of his or her names. Notice that Jacob did have a daughter named Dinah. She is the equivalent of Virgo. The four royal Persian stars can be equated with Reuben (Aquarius), Judah (Leo), Issachar (Taurus), and Dan (Scorpio).

In Genesis 49:1, we can read along and see that the twelve tribes/children of Jacob fit the twelve zodiacal constellations. Each of the eleven names is listed and has something to do with the constellation. (Dinah is excluded as women were not always considered worthy.)

Another interesting point is that the Old Testament has four major prophets—Isaiah, Jeremiah, Ezekiel, and Daniel. Then there are twelve minor prophets—Hosea, Joel, Amos, Obadiah, Jonah, Micah, Nahum, Habakkuk, Zephaniah, Haggai, Zechariah, and Malachi. Why twelve? Why four major prophets and why twelve minor? It seems as if they are humanizing the zodiac.

On the left is a map showing the twelve tribes of
Israel. They are named after ten of the children
of Jacob and two after the children of Joseph,
Ephraim and Manasseh. Why twelve? The
ancients knew there were twelve moons to a
year and the sun moved through twelve signs of
the zodiac. Jacob was a sun king, and his twelve
descendants were likened to the twelve signs of
the zodiac. Jerusalem was always considered
the center of the world, and looking north would
be where Naphtali and Zebulon are, both of
which can be paralleled with watery zodiacal
signs.

Fig. 11-4. The twelve tribes of Israel.

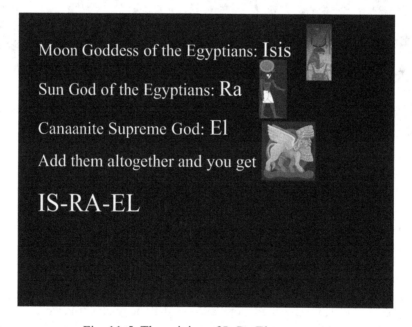

Fig. 11-5. The origins of Is Ra El.

It is interesting that, in Genesis 35:10, God changes Jacob's name to Israel. Add up the
trinity of ancient gods, and see what you get. Isis was the ancient moon goddess of the
Egyptians. Ra was the sun god of the Egyptians. El was the Canaanite supreme god. Put them
together, and we have the moon god plus the sun god plus the weather god. When combined all
together, Is-Ra-El is found.

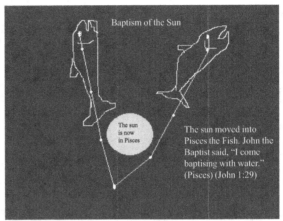

Fig. 11-6. John the Baptist.　　　　　Fig.11-7. The sun was in Pisces, the fish

The sun was in Pisces. Around two thousand years ago, about the same time as the birth of Christ, the sun was moving into Pisces on March 21, the vernal equinox or first day of spring. The symbol of Pisces is the two fish. John the Baptist (Fig. 11-6) said in John 1:26, "I come baptizing with water." Then in John 1:29, he says, "Behold the lamb of God." Have you ever wondered where all of the water symbology came from and baptizing? It was never done in the Old Testament. So why did they do it in the New Testament? Did someone realize the sun was in Pisces and it was a watery sign? Jesus ministry starts off as the Lamb of God and ends up eating fish, a perfect description of what the sun was doing. It was leaving the lamb of Aries and moving into the fish of Pisces.

Corona means crown.

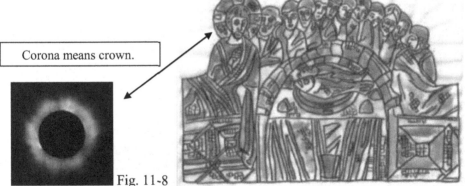

Fig. 11-8　　　　　　　　　　　　　　　　　　　　　　　　　　Fig. 11-9

In the tile mosaic on the right (Fig. 11-9) from AD 1000, we see Jesus with a halo and the cross shape upon it. Compare his halo to Fig. 11-8 and the solar corona, which means "crown." The ancients noticed that, during a total solar eclipse, the corona could be seen. Then look to the right of Jesus, and see the twelve disciples. On the table are the two fish and seven loaves of bread. In Mark 8:1 and Matthew 15:32, it mentions Jesus feeding four thousand with seven loaves and two fish. This entire mosaic reads like a sun movement symbolic story. Jesus is the sun in the sign of Pisces (two fish) moving through the twelve signs of the zodiac with seven loaves representing the seven visible celestial bodies.

The leaping fish above the doorway of St. Paul's Basilica in St. Paul, Minnesota. The fish is the symbol of Jesus because of ICHTHX, the secretive Greek letters that mean Jesus Christ God's Son, our Savior. Ichthys was the name of a "fish" in Greek. This was also a subliminal way to remember that the sun was in the sign of Pisces the Fish.

Fig. 11-10. Leaping fish of St. Paul's Basilica in St. Paul, Minnesota.

Each year, the sun goes on a one-year journey around the zodiac and then returns to the beginning spot along the zodiac.

Fig. 11-11. The sun in Pisces.

Fig. 11-12 The fish.

From our earthly perspective, it appears as if the sun is moving through all of the twelve signs of the zodiac. It is, in fact, Earth orbiting around the sun, which causes the apparent movement. In this viewpoint, we see the sun is in Pisces. This alignment occurred on the spring equinox of March 21 in the year 0. The sun was precessing from Aries into Pisces on that date. The symbology of going from the lamb into the fish (Fig. 11-12) would be appropriate symbols seen in the Christian religion, where Jesus was introduced as the Lamb of God. And then after resurrection, the first thing he does is eat a broiled fish. In the next hundred or so years, the sun will next move into Aquarius and then continue along its annual journey.

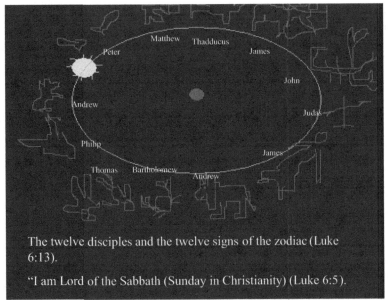

The twelve disciples and the twelve signs of the zodiac (Luke 6:13).

"I am Lord of the Sabbath (Sunday in Christianity) (Luke 6:5).

Fig. 11-13. The zodiac and the twelve disciples.

Once again, by adding the names of the twelve disciples, we can see how they fit into with zodiacal constellations. Peter the fisherman is besides Pisces to associate with the fish symbol. Matthew is with Aquarius and the water jar. John is shown with Scorpio and Judas with Libra. Perhaps it might be more appropriate to switch them around, giving Judas the dubious association with the stinger of a scorpion.

The twenty-four elders mentioned in Revelation 11:16

The Twelve Children of Jacob, the Twelve Disciples of Christ, the Twelve Zodiacal Signs.

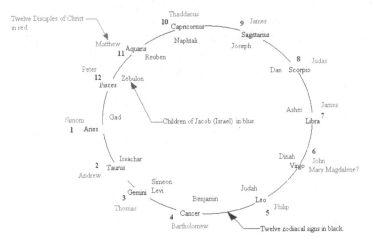

Jacob and Jesus are both like sun gods moving through their twelve signs of the zodiac. Jacob is like the sun with his twelve children and Jesus like the sun with his twelve disciples.

Fig. 11-14. The trio of twelves.

107

The twelve children of Jacob, the twelve zodiacal signs, and the twelve disciples of Christ are compared. Twenty-four elders surround the throne as in Revelation 11:16. In Luke 1:33, it says, "Jesus will reign over the house of Jacob for ever, and of his kingdom there will be no end." That is what the sun does.

Fig. 11-15. Old painting reveals sun god in center.

Here is a very interesting painting from AD 700 that shows in the center a young man without a beard riding on a chariot pulled by four horses. (See Fig. 11-16.) The cross identifies him with Jesus, though he could be Apollo or Helios. Up until the fourth century, Jesus was often depicted without a beard. Twelve naked virgins surround the central Christ-like figure (see enlargement below). These virgins could have to do with the lunar cycles and a woman's monthly menstrual cycle. Virgin sacrifice is mentioned in Judges 11:31 and 39. On the second ring are the twelve disciples of Jesus. Finally, the outer ring is of the twelve signs of the zodiac. So here we see a relationship between the central humanized sun figure pulled by four horses, lunar sacrifice, and then the surrounding twelve disciples and the twelve signs of the zodiac. That is astrology in action.

Fig. 11-16. A youthful sun god in the middle.

Chapter Twelve
The Changes in the Zodiac and Precession

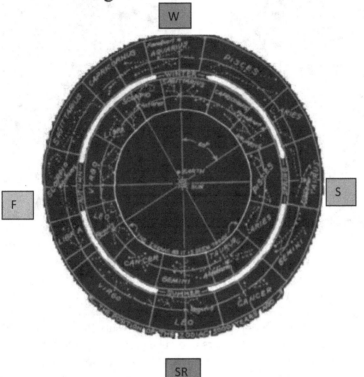

Fig. 12-1. Changes in the zodiac.

This illustration will help you understand why there has been such a dramatic shift in the zodiac in the past five thousand years. This science neither the ancients nor their religion could explain. Look at the light-green S of spring on the right side, and note it is near Taurus. That is where the sun was located on March 21, the first day of spring in 3000 BC. Then look to the left of Taurus, and see the word "spring" a little more to the left and the constellation of Pisces. That is where the sun is now located on the first day of spring. Then move to the bottom, and note the dark-green SR is in Leo. That was on June 21, 3000 BC, the first day of summer. It is now in Gemini (located right above Leo) on that same date. Why is this happening? There has been a sixty-degree shift in the sun's position. The illustration below shows where the sun was at on AD 0 as it was entering Pisces. Today, because of precession at A.D.2000, it is leaving Pisces

Fig. 12-2. Precession of the sun in 5000 years.

What is precession?

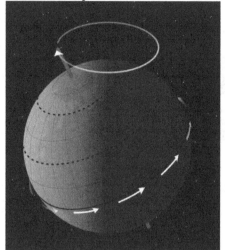

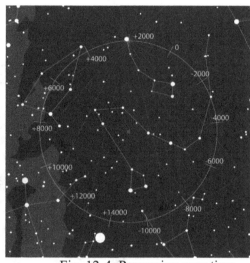

Fig. 12-3. Earth and precession   Fig. 12-4. Precession over time

Precession is due to Earth's wobble. It is only very slight, but it is enough to precess the movement of the sun westward by one degree every seventy-two years. Hipparchus of ancient Greece seems to have correctly observed precession in 127 BC. On the upper left illustration, see the top analogy. The Earth is wobbling as it turns. The image on the upper right shows the ever-changing pole, caused again by precession. In 12,500 years (look at +14000), the North Pole will be near Vega, as it was 12,500 years ago. The complete cycle for the shift in the polar axis takes 25,920 years, the same amount of time for the sun to move completely around the zodiac. You might find it curious that Osiris had seventy-two accomplices involved in his murder. In India, the base number of all the yugas, or divine epochs, is the number seventy-two. Moses has seventy elders of Israel help him in Numbers 11:16. Jesus had seventy or seventy-two disciples come to help him in Luke 10:1. One of the promises in Islam for good deeds is seventy-two virgins. As you can see, the ancient world knew something about this number seventy-two, though they attribute it to superstition and religion, as it was not very easily explained without science.

Fig. 12-5. The seventy or seventy-two apostles for Christ in Luke 10:1.

Fig. 12-6. The Antikythera astronomical clock (Photo by Mogi).

Did the ancients really understand celestial mechanics? Here is evidence they did. This very ancient clock was found in a Mediterranean Sea shipwreck in the early twentieth century, which most likely sunk back around 76 BC, near the island of Antikythera south of Greece. It gives us clues to the knowledge that the ancients had about the movement of the sun along the zodiac and the travel of the stars and planets. Archimedes of Syracuse, who had a grand knowledge of engineering, mathematics, astronomy, and the use of mechanics, may have built the clock. It could calculate the position of the sun, moon, and planets. It accurately told, to the hour, the dates of solar and lunar eclipses. It could also calculate the eighteen-year saros period, which is the repeating period of a total solar eclipse. This is very important evidence that the eighteen-year disappearance of Jesus perhaps was borrowed

Fig. 12-7. The clock's interior.

This is a photograph of the Antikythera clockworks. It truly looks like a modern-day assemblage. By using a system of mechanical gears and cogs, the device could be used to calculate many astronomical functions. This information is additional evidence that the ancients did have a great deal of knowledge on astronomy, but much of it was lost.

Chapter 13

The Misunderstood Astronomy behind the Birth and Life of Jesus

The morning star that heralded the birth of Jesus could have been Jupiter or Venus. The light rivaled the rising sun. Jupiter means Zeus, or Zeus-Pater, which means God the Father (Matt. 2:1).

Fig. 13-1. The 'star' may have been Jupiter

Was Jupiter the rising star? Matthew 2:1 mentions a rising star that the wise men from the East followed. That star could have been the Planet Jupiter. Its name means Zeus Pater, which translates into "God the Father." This could have been seen as a rival to the rising sun and was interpreted to herald in the coming sun. The birth of Jesus is merely another interpolation of the sun rising around the winter solstice.

When they had heard the king, they set out; and there, ahead of them, went the star that they had seen at its rising, until it stopped over the place where the child was. When they saw that the star had stopped, they were overwhelmed with joy (Matt. 2:9).

Fig. 13-2. Matthew 2:9 and the star stopped.

People have long looked to the night sky for a sign or portent of something yet to come. This is what astrology is based upon, foretelling events and predicting outcomes based on positions of stars and planets in what zodiacal sign they were located. The Matthew 2:9 story tells of some wise men setting out and following a star they saw rising. They followed it until it stopped over the place where the child was born. There is only one problem.

Stars cannot stop. That is impossible. It would mean the Earth would have to stop turning.

Fig. 13-3. Stars can't stop.

One of the problems with the Matthew story is believing that stars can stop, as in Matthew 2:9. We are led to believe that is what happened. The star stopped in the night sky, but this is impossible because it means Earth would have to stop turning. The only reason stars rise and fall is because of Earth's turning. In biblical times, they did not understand this concept. They thought Earth was stationary and everything moved around it.

One explanation could be …

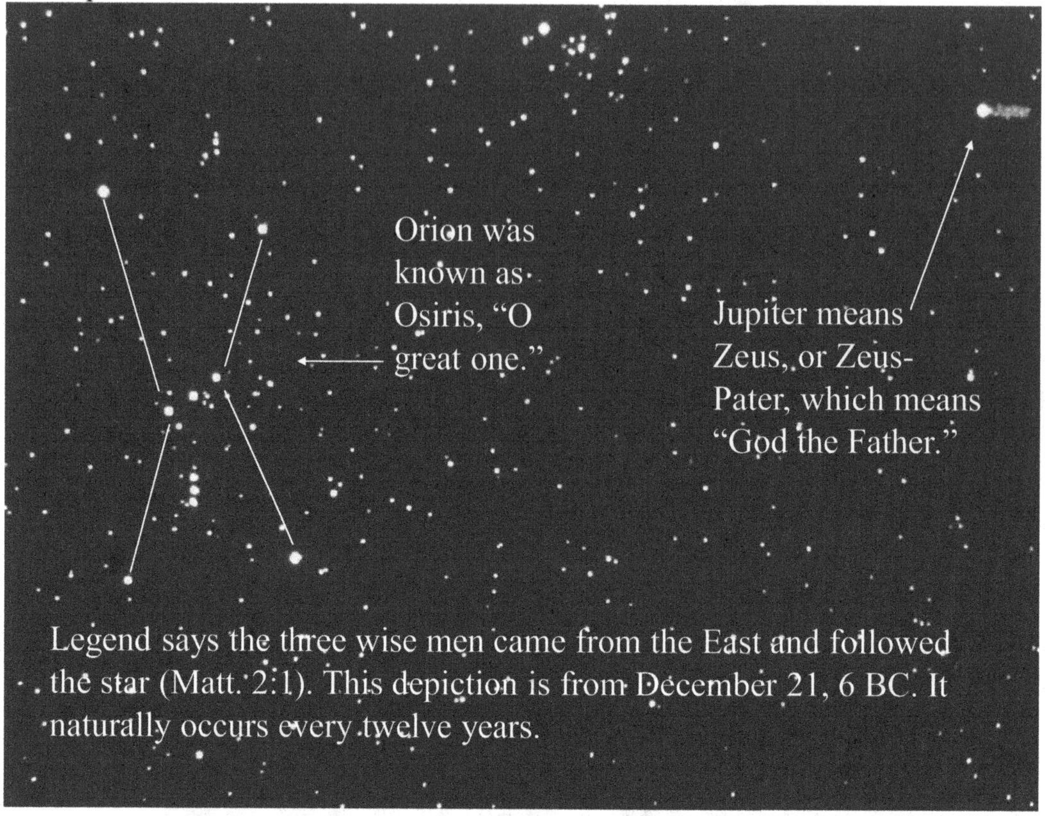

Orion was known as Osiris, "O great one."

Jupiter means Zeus, or Zeus-Pater, which means "God the Father."

Legend says the three wise men came from the East and followed the star (Matt. 2:1). This depiction is from December 21, 6 BC. It naturally occurs every twelve years.

Fig. 13-4. Orion's belt

Could the three wise men have been misinterpreted as Orion's belt? For the last two thousand years, the constellation of Orion is high in the winter sky. It has three belt stars in the middle of it. They have been long associated with the great one, or O Great One,[2] Osiris, the ancient god of the Egyptians. About seven thousand years ago, the sun would have been above Orion at the spring equinox. They turned Osiris, or Orion to the Greeks, into a god.

Above, we see a depiction from 6 BC that is of Osiris and the three belt stars and the Planet Jupiter in Taurus/Aries. They might have thought that the three belt stars followed the star that is, in fact, Jupiter. Jupiter has long been considered a god, as that is what Zeus means (Deus or deity) and Pater (Father). Thus, we have Zeus-Pater. The problem is that this event happens often, every twelve years, so it is nothing special unless the untrained eye of astrology is involved.

---

[2] *Egyptian Book of the Dead*, 121, 151.

Tales from the Arabian Magi gave gifts to the sun. The three belt stars of Osiris were known as the three kings. They symbolized the pharaoh's riches of gold, frankincense, and myrrh. The three belt stars were also known as the shining pearls.

Fig. 13-5. The three belt stars of Orion.

The three belt stars of Orion were associated with the Magi or "magic way" long before the time of Christ. Many ancient tales revolve around them. Tales from the Arabian Magi giving gifts to the sun and symbology of the Pharaoh's riches of gold, frankincense, and myrrh precede the Christian idea. One theory is that the three belt stars are replicated in the three pyramids of Giza, of which one of them is offset, just like the far right belt star.

If the planet Jupiter were in Taurus, as is shown above the right hand of Osiris, then someone in ancient times could have thought that the alignment with the three belt stars of Osiris and the brightest star in the night sky, Sirius, had some kind of significance. For one thing, that alignment points toward the rising sun.

115

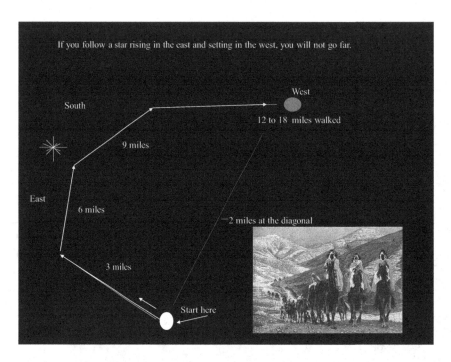

Fig. 13-6.What if you followed a star?

Let's say you want to replicate the Matthew story by following a rising star. It would be coming up in the east, and you would head that direction. Then, as Earth turned, it would rise higher until it began to head west. Therefore, you would be walking in a large U-like configuration. It would be very wasteful to do this. A lot of extra energy and time would be required to reach a destination. In one night, a journey would take us three miles east, three miles south, three miles southwest, and three miles west. That is a total of twelve miles, but it would only be about two miles at the diagonal. This would be very wasteful, and the ancient world would never do such foolishness.

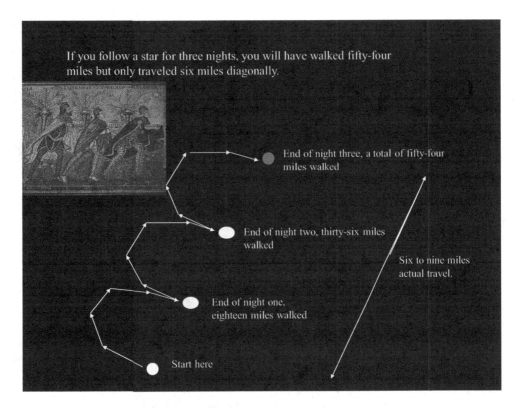

Fig. 13-7. Following a star for three days and nights.

Let's say you were really energetic and you and the camels went eighteen miles in one night. Then for three nights, it would have accumulated into fifty-four miles of travel. However, you really only went six to nine miles on the diagonal.

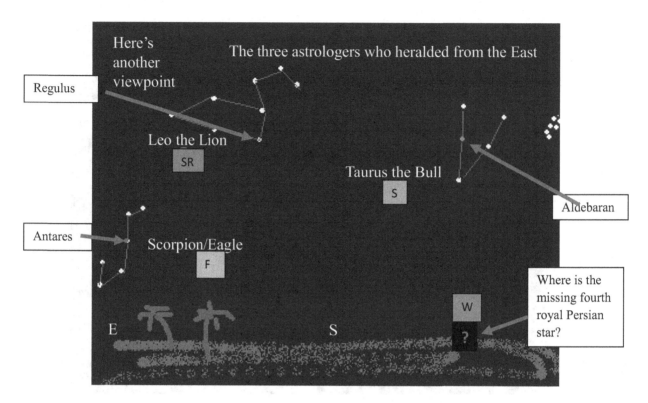

Fig. 13-8. Another explanation

Perhaps there is another way of looking at the story of the three wise men. They could have been three of the four royal Persian stars. On any given night, one might be able to see three royal Persian stars at nearly the same time. It depends on how expansive one's horizon is. In this depiction, we see Aldebaran in Taurus, Regulus in Leo, and Antares in Scorpio. So perhaps, the three wise men is an interpolation of the rising three royal Persian stars in the East. The missing star is the one that cannot be seen and therefore becomes a mysterious Christ-like being.

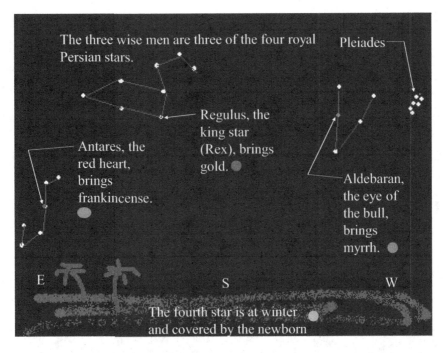

The three wise men are three of the four royal Persian stars.

Pleiades

Regulus, the king star (Rex), brings gold.

Antares, the red heart, brings frankincense.

Aldebaran, the eye of the bull, brings myrrh.

E   S   W

The fourth star is at winter and covered by the newborn

Fig. 13-9. Three wise men?

Gold is Regulus, frankincense is Antares, and myrrh is Aldebaran. The association of the three gifts by the three wise men and the three constellations can be explained as associations. It might go way back to pre-Christian myths. Adonis was born from a myrrh tree. He would rise out of the Earth on the vernal equinox/spring (when the sun was in Taurus) to unite with his lover Aphrodite. The growing Adonic (Easter?) lilies are a sign of his ascent. The constellation of Taurus was where the sun was located five thousand years ago on March 21.

The gold symbology of the star Regulus as gold is the crown that kings wear. Regulus is known as the kingly star (Rex). The hot sun of gold was at its highest in Leo on June 21, 3000 BC. Antares, the red star, was considered the heart of a scorpion in Scorpio, much like frankincense is a scented red powder. Gold and frankincense are mentioned in Isaiah 60:6.

Where is the fourth missing royal Persian star? The fourth star (Aquarius) is covered by the newborn sun, where the baby Jesus is yet to be born.

119

The sun is in Aquarius on December 21, 3000 BC. The winter solstice

Winter! [w]

Fig. 13-10. Image courtesy of Stellarium.

The remaining royal Persian star of the three would be Aquarius. The three zodiacal signs of Taurus, Leo, and Scorpio were shown, and this would be the fourth zodiacal sign, where the sun is located on December 21. It would not be visible, but it is the constellation of Aquarius, symbolized as Matthew, the man with the water jar.

A curious connection occurs with Jesus and water. In John 7:37 (New Revised Standard Version), Jesus says, "Let anyone who is thirsty come to me, and let the one who believes in me drink." John 7:38 reads, "Scripture has said, out of the believers heart shall flow rivers of living water." The only scriptures around when Jesus, who was a Jew, was quoted as saying this were from the Old Testament, and no such quotation like this can be found anywhere in it.

On December 21, the winter solstice, the sun does appears to stop. Solstice literally means "sun stops."

SE

Fig. 13:11. Solstice

At the birth of Christ, the Bible says a star stopped above the place of his birth. Stars cannot stop, but the sun does appear to stop in its southerly movement along the eastern horizon on December 21, the winter solstice. The word "solstice" literally means "sun stops." The infant sun goes the furthest south on that day. In the biblical story, Joseph and Mary flee south to Egypt right after his birth.

The sun was "born" on a cold winter morning in a cave or a manger, surrounded by the animals of the zodiac (Luke 2:12).

Winter Solstice

Fig 13-12. The 'birth' of the sun

In Luke 2:12, Jesus is born in a manger, a place for animals. This is much the same as the sun passing through the zodiac, which means "the path of animals." Jesus becomes a personification of the sun, so his movements mimic the sun's. There has long been a misnomer by the ancients that the sun goes into a cave at night and rises out of the cave in the morning. In fact, in Ecclesiastes 1:5, it says, "The sun rises and the sun goes down, and hastens to the place where it rises." Hastens? Like it runs through a tunnel?

121

The sun goes farthest south and is a "newborn" on December 21. There is no more room for the sun to move. Three days and three nights later, the sun starts to move back north. The baby Jesus was born on December 25, and his family moved south.

SE

Fig. 13-13. Newborn sun.

In the biblical narrative, Jesus is born in a manger because there is no more room for him in the inn. This is also much the same as the apparent motion of sun. The sun cannot go any further south because it has reached the point of solstice. It actually takes about three days for the sun to be noticed to move northward. Therefore, about December 25, the sun is again moving back north. Jesus goes south to Egypt and then returns north to Nazareth, much the same as the sun's movement.

The "baby" sun then returns north (Matt. 2:21). It does this every year.

Fig. 13-14. Baby sun

Each year, the "newborn sun," after the winter solstice, starts to move back north. The baby sun is much like the baby Jesus. It moves north like Jesus goes north to Nazareth. The actual reason that the sun appears to do this is because of the orbit of Earth around the sun.

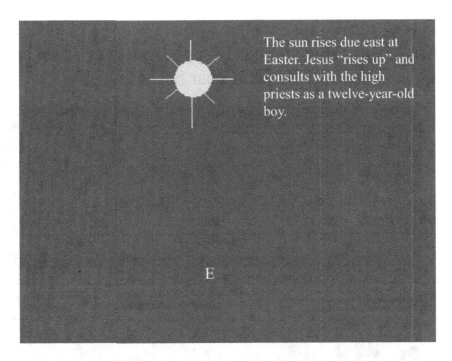

The sun rises due east at Easter. Jesus "rises up" and consults with the high priests as a twelve-year-old boy.

E

Fig. 13-15. The sun rises east at Easter.

The sun rises dues east on March 21, around Passover and Easter. On March 21, it is the vernal equinox. The sun rises due east on that day and sets due west. The Passover event is always held on the first full moon after the vernal equinox. So it had something to do with the rising sun in the east and the full moon. King Solomon's Temple faced due east. It was built on the rock where Abraham would slay Isaac. It faced east. It was the perfect spot to observe the eastern springtime rising of the sun.

The interesting aspect to the story of Jesus is how many of his events have parallels with something to do with the sun and manipulations of basic astronomy. This therefore brings one to ponder the possibility that the ancients did not fully comprehend what the sun truly was, nor understand its motions, and they personified it into a humanized form.

Chapter 14

The Amazing Eighteen-Year Disappearance of Jesus and the Sun's Eighteen-Year Saros Cycle

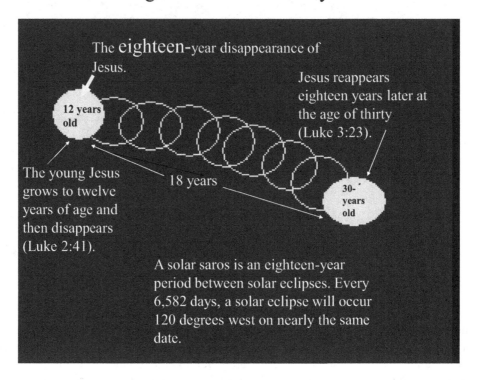

Fig. 14-1. The eighteen-year disappearance of Jesus.

Where did Jesus go from the age of twelve to thirty years of age? This eighteen-year disappearance of Jesus can once again be explained, just like the other astronomical misunderstandings, as a personification of the sun's movement. The sun goes through an eighteen-year cycle called the saros period. Every eighteen years and eleven days, a total eclipse occurs 120 degrees to the west of the previous one. Because the ancients humanized the sun into the persona of Jesus, he disappears, just like the sun does every saros period.

The sun repeats an eclipse cycle every eighteen years by shifting 120 degrees westward.   .

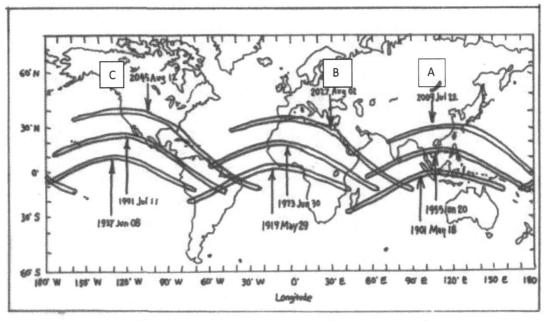

Fig. 14-2. Saros patterns shift 120 degrees westward.

Here you can see the repeating pattern of the saros period. Look at figure A, and see that the eclipse of July 22, 2009, over China and India shifts 120 degrees westward and eighteen years later to B over the Mediterranean on August 2, 2027. Then look at C over the United States on August 12, 2045, and see this was eighteen years later than B. See the same shifting on the middle saros patterns starting on the right side with 1955, then to 1973, and again eighteen years later to July 1991. The bottom level of the saros paths also demonstrates this pattern of shifting 120 degrees westward.

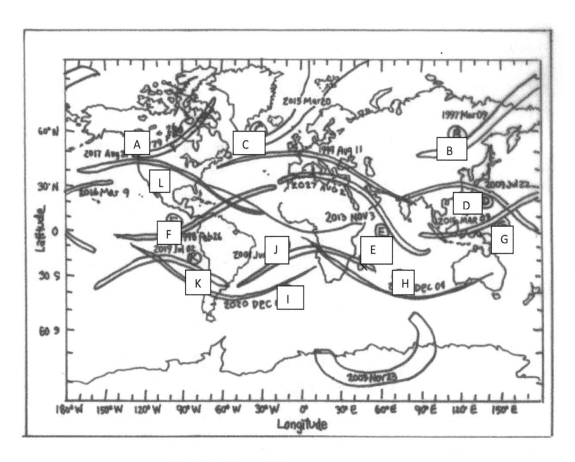

Fig. 14-3. More shifting saros patterns.

Here are more shifting eighteen-year saros eclipse patterns. At A, I witnessed the February 26, 1979, total eclipse of the sun in Riverton, Manitoba. This saros period was repeated in 1997 at B and then will again occur in 2015 at C. You can see that F was repeated at G, and J repeated at K and H at I. We are all looking forward to seeing the next total solar eclipse across the United States at L on August 21, 2017.

126

The forty-day mystery can be explained as part of an ancient solar calendar.

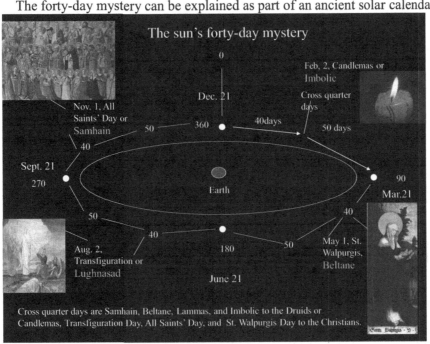

Fig. 14-4. The forty-/fifty-day cycle.

The forty-day and forty-night period is used many times in the Bible. Moses spent forty days up on Mount Sinai, and he spent forty days in the wilderness. Jesus spent forty days in the wilderness. Where did this number forty come from? The ancient Druids followed a calendar that started with the winter solstice, went forty days to Imbolic (Groundhog Day), and then went fifty days to March 21 (spring). Then it went forty days to May Day (Beltane) and then fifty days to June 21 (summer solstice). Then it went forty days to August 1 (Lugnhasad) and fifty days to September 21 (autumnal equinox). Then it went forty days to Halloween/All Saints' Day and fifty days to December 21.

In the Bible, Jesus spends forty days in the wilderness and then begins his ministry. After the crucifixion, he disappears for fifty days of Pentecost and then returns for the resurrection.

The ministry of Jesus is like the annual movement of the sun through the four seasons.

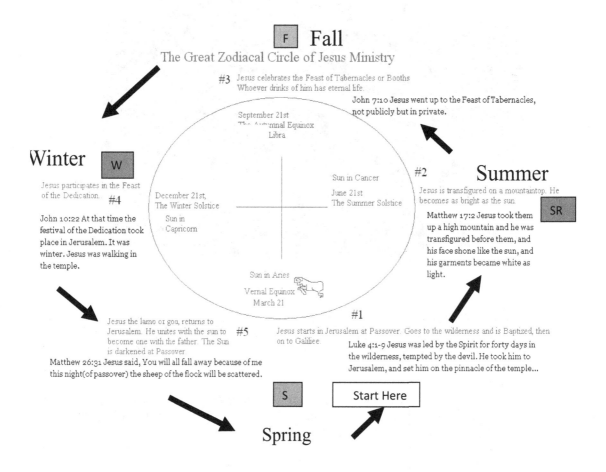

Fig. 14-5. The sun and Jesus movement.

The entire story of Jesus is likened to the movement of the sun and the changing seasons. He is born around the winter solstice. He is seen at age twelve around Passover, disappears for eighteen years, reappears again around Passover, and spends forty days in the wilderness near Jerusalem. He then goes northward along the River Jordan, around the waters of Galilee, and up north to the mountain where he is transfigured. He then returns south to Jerusalem where he is crucified on Passover. His movement mimics the cyclic movement of the sun, a natural process.

Chapter 15

The Story of Jesus is like the Story of the Sun's Annual Movement along the Horizon during the Year

In the following depiction, we see the sun rise relative to Jerusalem during the year. It rises in the southeast during winter and moves northward until the summer solstice. Jesus does much the same thing.

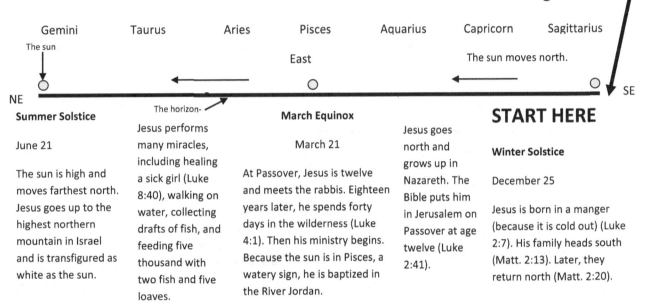

Gemini　　Taurus　　Aries　　Pisces　　Aquarius　　Capricorn　　Sagittarius

The sun

East

The sun moves north.

NE

SE

Summer Solstice

The horizon

March Equinox

START HERE

June 21

Jesus performs many miracles, including healing a sick girl (Luke 8:40), walking on water, collecting drafts of fish, and feeding five thousand with two fish and five loaves.

March 21

At Passover, Jesus is twelve and meets the rabbis. Eighteen years later, he spends forty days in the wilderness (Luke 4:1). Then his ministry begins. Because the sun is in Pisces, a watery sign, he is baptized in the River Jordan.

Jesus goes north and grows up in Nazareth. The Bible puts him in Jerusalem on Passover at age twelve (Luke 2:41).

Winter Solstice

December 25

The sun is high and moves farthest north. Jesus goes up to the highest northern mountain in Israel and is transfigured as white as the sun.

Jesus is born in a manger (because it is cold out) (Luke 2:7). His family heads south (Matt. 2:13). Later, they return north (Matt. 2:20).

Fig. 15-1 (above) and 15-2 (below)

After the transfiguration, Jesus moves south, just like the hot sun does.

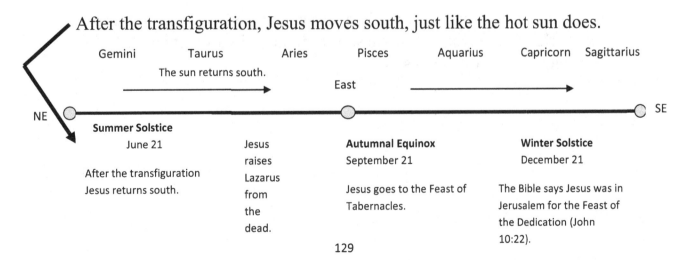

Gemini　　Taurus　　Aries　　Pisces　　Aquarius　　Capricorn　Sagittarius

The sun returns south.

East

NE

SE

Summer Solstice

June 21

After the transfiguration Jesus returns south.

Jesus raises Lazarus from the dead.

Autumnal Equinox
September 21

Jesus goes to the Feast of Tabernacles.

Winter Solstice
December 21

The Bible says Jesus was in Jerusalem for the Feast of the Dedication (John 10:22).

Jesus spends the winter in Jerusalem and then moves out of the city and returns to Jerusalem on Passover, riding upon a foal. He is crucified upon the symbol of the sun's annual movement, the crux. The story of Jesus is much like the changing position of the sun during the year.

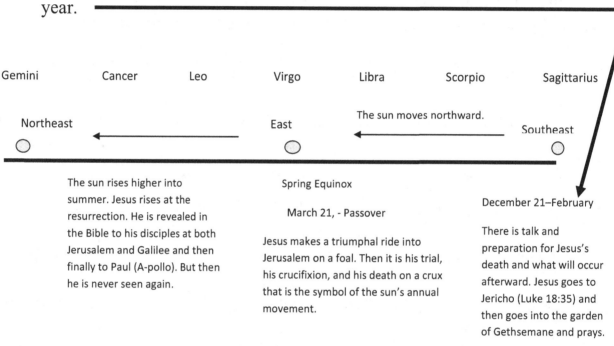

Gemini	Cancer	Leo	Virgo	Libra	Scorpio	Sagittarius

Northeast   East   The sun moves northward.   Southeast

The sun rises higher into summer. Jesus rises at the resurrection. He is revealed in the Bible to his disciples at both Jerusalem and Galilee and then finally to Paul (A-pollo). But then he is never seen again.

Spring Equinox

March 21, - Passover

Jesus makes a triumphal ride into Jerusalem on a foal. Then it is his trial, his crucifixion, and his death on a crux that is the symbol of the sun's annual movement.

December 21–February

There is talk and preparation for Jesus's death and what will occur afterward. Jesus goes to Jericho (Luke 18:35) and then goes into the garden of Gethsemane and prays.

Fig. 15-3. The journey of Jesus can be compared to the journey of the sun.

Just remember that Jerusalem was considered to be the center of the world. The movement of the sun from the point of view of Jerusalem is what was considered.

Chapter 16

The Sun Is in Pisces and Jesus Loves Water

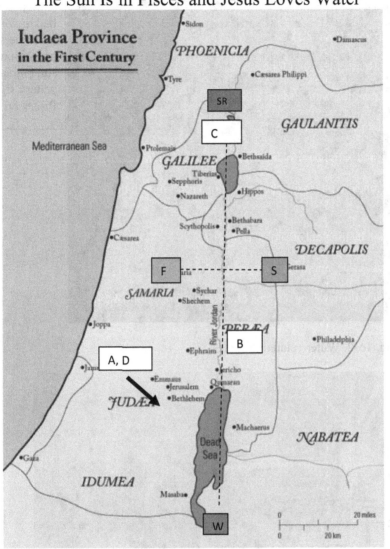

Iudaea Province in the First Century

The ministry of Jesus follows the water. He starts out at in Jerusalem (A) and then moves over to the Jordan River (B). Then he follows the water up to the Sea of Galilee (C). He is transfigured and returns to D, where he is crucified. This is identical to what the sun's movement does. At winter, it rises in the south. Than at the equinox, it rises east of Jerusalem, moves north to the summer solstice, and then heads south to the winter solstice.

Fig. 16-1. Follow the water.

The story of Jesus involves baptism, which was not done as a ritual for acceptance into the Jewish faith in the Old Testament. Baptism was done in the New Testament because the sun was now in the sign of water, Pisces. Jesus is baptized and follows the Jordan River northward to the Sea of Galilee, where he walks on water, calms the water, turns water into wine, cures a blind man by the pool of Siloam, and drowns pigs in water. Finally, while on the cross, he is stabbed by the spear of Longinus, and out comes water. All of these involve water in his symbology. This is once again because the sun no longer was in the symbol of the lamb. It was now in the symbol of the fish, Pisces. Notice how the journey of Jesus is like the four seasons and locations of the sun, and makes an imaginary crucifix shape over Israel.

Miracles of Jesus that have to do with water because the sun was now in Pisces on March 21, AD 0

1. His chief disciple was Peter, a fisherman.

2. He turns water into wine (John 2:1).

3. He walks on water (Matt. 14:22 and John 6:18).

4. He stills a tempest over the water (Matt. 8:23).

5. He provides a draught of fishes (Luke 5:1).

6. He feeds five thousand with two fish and five loaves of bread (Matt. 14:15).

7. He offers tribute money to pay taxes obtained from a fish's mouth (Matt. 17:24).

8. He cures a blind man by the Pool of Siloam (John 9:7).

9. Soldier pierced Jesus's side, and water came out (John 19:34).

10. "The water I will give them will be a spring of water gushing" (John 4:14).

Here are some more of the water miracles in the Christ story. They had to with misunderstandings of astronomy, of the sun being in the watery sign of Pisces on March 21.

Fig. 16-2. Water-related miracles.

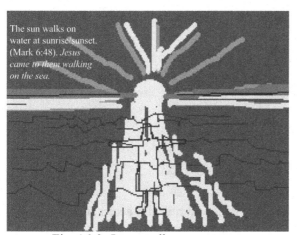

Fig. 16-3. Jesus walks on water.

Fig. 16-4. Water miracles.

Jesus walks on water like the sun reflects on water (Matt. 14:25 and Mark 6:48). Jesus washed the feet of the disciples with water (John 13).

132

Under the sun, the sick are healed, those who appear dead or are cold are warmed and brought back to life (Luke 4:38).

Fig. 16-5. Luke 4-40 reads; "As the sun was setting…"

The Bible says that, with Jesus, the sick are healed and dead are brought back to life. (John 11:38). This is also what the warmth of the sun can do. Psalm 84:11 reads, "For the Lord God is a sun and shield."

The ministry of Jesus follows the water. He is born near Jerusalem. He heads south, returns north, and follows the Jordan River up to the Sea of Galilee, where many miracles are performed. He then does a circuit around the lake, heads north to the highest mountain, and then heads south back to Jerusalem. He mimics the sun.

Fig. 16-6.
The journey of Jesus follows the water.

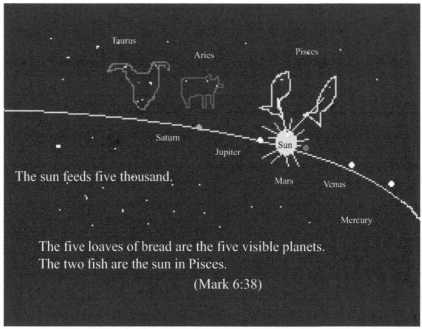

Fig. 16-7. Loaves and fishes

Jesus feeds five thousand with two fish and five loaves of bread. This miracle could be allegorical of the five known planets and the zodiacal symbol of Pisces the Fish.

Fig. 16-8. Praise Jesus and the Sun

Science has taught us that all of life on Earth is made from the sun. See the similarity of John 1:3–6, "All things were made through Jesus" story and the "All things were made from the sun" story by just interchanging the words "Jesus" and "the sun."

Chapter 17

The Mission of Jesus and the Sun's Annual Journey

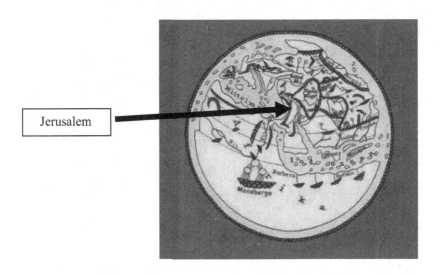

Fig. 17-1. The center of the world

Jerusalem was considered the center of the world to the Jews and Christians. All roads led to Jerusalem.

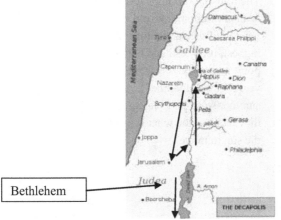

The movement of Jesus and the movement of the sun, relative to Jerusalem. He is born south of Jerusalem (in Bethlehem) around the winter solstice. Then his family goes south to Egypt. Then they return north to Nazareth for his childhood. Then he goes south to Jerusalem on Passover at age twelve. Then he disappears for eighteen years. He reappears in Jerusalem at Passover again at age thirty. Jesus goes east to the Jordan River and follows it up to Galilee. He is transfigured. Then he heads south to Jerusalem and is crucified at Passover.

Fig. 17-2. Jesus's movement

The story of Jesus's journey is like the movement of the sun as seen from Jerusalem. The sun is south of Jerusalem in Bethlehem on December 25, the birth of Jesus. Then he goes south into Egypt, just like the sun appears to move south. Then in the spring, he moves north to Nazareth and grows up. His missions are around the Sea of Galilee, and he goes far north of it on June 21, the summer solstice, and is transfigured. Eventually, he moves south back to Jerusalem, just like the sun appears to do.

The sun moves to its highest point on June 21, the summer solstice. Jesus goes to the highest mountaintop.

Mark 9:3 (the transfiguration of Jesus) says, "His clothes became dazzling white, as no one on earth could bleach them."

Summer

Fig. 17-3. Matt.17-1 "His face shone like the sun.."

In the Bible, Mark tells us about the transfiguration of Jesus. The sun moves to its highest northward position during the summer time of year. It is at its very brightest, and Mark 9:3 suggests an incredible likeness of Jesus to the summer sun. Of course, no one on Earth could … because it is not on Earth. It is the sun!

The transfiguration of Jesus is an anthropomorphized version of the sun being at its highest, brightest, and hottest point in the sky during the year. We call that the summer solstice. Long ago, they had no clue what caused the sun to move.

Fig. 17-4. The transfiguration.

After the summer solstice. the sun moves south, and Jesus does the same.

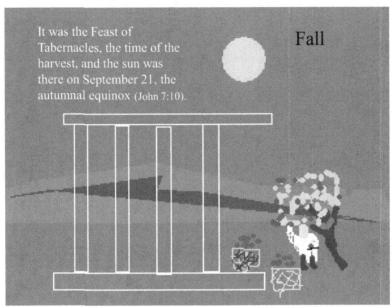

Fig. 17-5 Fall

Jesus was at the Feast of Tabernacles in the fall when the sun is at the equinox on September 21 and it starts heading south. So did Jesus in John 7:10.

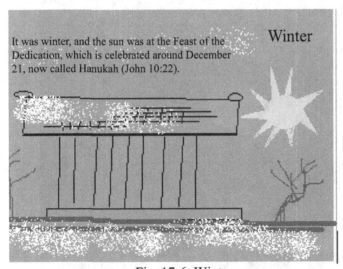

Fig. 17-6. Winter

It is winter, and Jesus was in Jerusalem to celebrate the Feast of the Dedication (John 10:22).

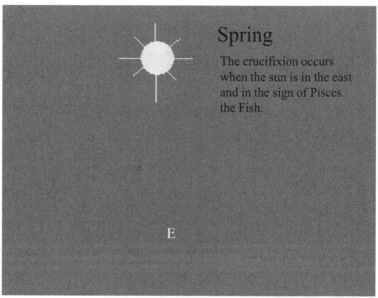

Fig. 17-7. Spring

The crucifixion occurs at springtime. The sun is now at the equinox and heading northward into the northern part of our sky. Jesus goes full circle, like the sun, and returns to Jerusalem.

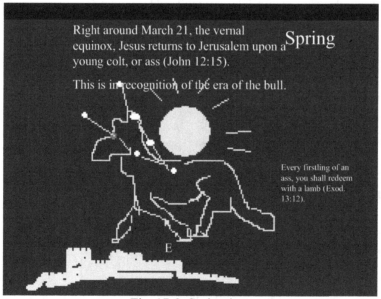

Fig. 17-8. Springtime

Jesus rides in on a hooved animal. As it says in John 12:15, Jesus rides into Jerusalem upon a colt or, some say, an ass (a hooved quadruped). This could be symbolic of the end of the era of the Bull. John the Baptist deemed Jesus as the Lamb of God, and he is about to be sacrificed to usher in Pisces.

Fig. 17-9. The lamb of Spring

John the Baptist introduces Jesus as the lamb. Just as the lamb was used as the Passover feast for the Hebrews, Jesus's blood and body was identified with the Lamb of God. The sun too had moved from Aries the Ram/Lamb and was now in Pisces.

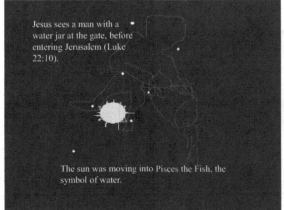

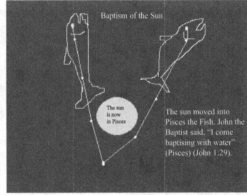

Fig. 17-10. Jesus see the man with the water jar.   Fig. 17-11. Jesus and the age of Pisces.

Just before Jesus enters Jerusalem, he sees a man with a water jar at the gate (Luke 22:10). Could this imply something to do with the sun being born at the winter solstice in Aquarius, the man with the water jar? Or does it have something to do with the sun being in the sign of Pisces? He is now about to enter the sign of water.

Chapter 18

Passover and the Easter Resurrection

Passover is held on the first full moon after the vernal equinox. Easter is held on the first Sunday after the first full moon after the vernal equinox.

Fig. 18-1. Passover

There can never be a total solar eclipse of the sun on Passover, but there can be a total lunar eclipse. Between the years AD 26 and 34, Easter and Passover did not fall on the same date as when Christ was alive, so there could not have been a total solar eclipse on Passover at the time of Jesus.

Though the New Testament is not specific, the resurrection occurs after the Jewish Sabbath, which is always on a Saturday. The Christian story of Jesus's resurrection occurs on a Sunday. Is that any wonder? He is a sun allegory! Sunday is the first day of the week, and it is dedicated to the sun.

The Babylonians had a moon god named Sin, the son of Enlil and Ninlil. He was called "the father of the gods" and rode around on a winged bull. He was considered as "the creator of all things."

Sin is shown as a moon symbol between the high priest and a goddess.

Fig. 18-2. The moon god Sin.

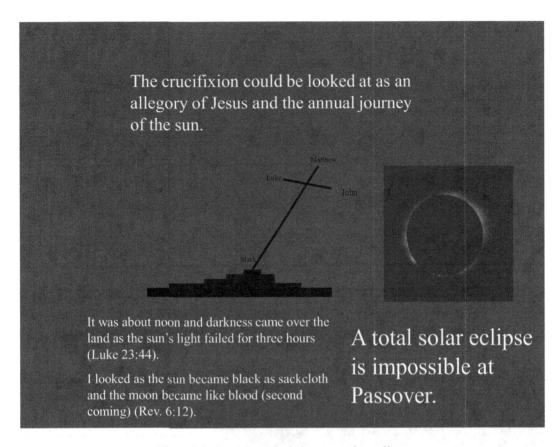

The crucifixion could be looked at as an allegory of Jesus and the annual journey of the sun.

It was about noon and darkness came over the land as the sun's light failed for three hours (Luke 23:44).

I looked as the sun became black as sackcloth and the moon became like blood (second coming) (Rev. 6:12).

A total solar eclipse is impossible at Passover.

Fig. 18-3. Passover can't have a solar eclipse.

Easter is held on the first Sunday after the first full moon after March 21st, the vernal equinox. Jesus was crucified at Passover, not Easter. The sun could not turn dark from a total eclipse at the crucifixion because a total solar eclipse at Passover would be impossible.

Once again, Luke 23:45 says the sun's light failed for three hours during the crucifixion. This could not be a total solar eclipse. A total solar eclipse cannot occur on Passover because it is only held at full moon. It could be a major thunderstorm or sandstorm, but then, why wasn't that recorded? Most ancient Bibles read in Luke 23:45, "There was a solar eclipse." (Pap. 75, Aleph. B.C.L. Coptic, WH, R.V., A.S.V., R.S.V., and N.E.B., all mention there being a solar eclipse.)

Luke 23:45 original passage seems to have been removed or modified over the centuries to read that the sun's light failed or was darkened. This is strictly against God's Word mentioned in Matthew 5:18 and Revelation 22:18–19 that, if anyone adds or takes away one jot from the words of the Bible, God will take away from them.

The other aspect to remember is a contradiction to what is written in Revelation 6:12. "I looked as the sun became black as sackcloth and the moon became like blood." This describes a total solar eclipse and a total lunar eclipse. The two cannot occur at the same time. That is impossible. They would have to be at least two weeks apart from each other.

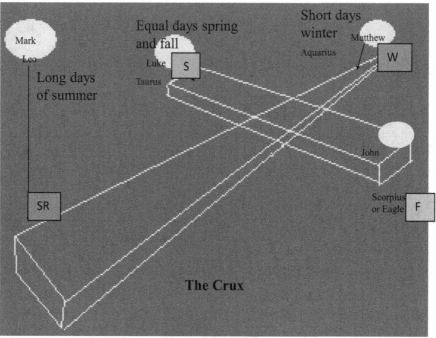

Fig. 18-4. Crux shape explained

The crux is a symbol of the sun's movement during the year. The short axis near Matthew represents the short days of winter. The long axis to Mark represents the long days of summer. The Luke to John axis represents the equinox, equal days and nights.

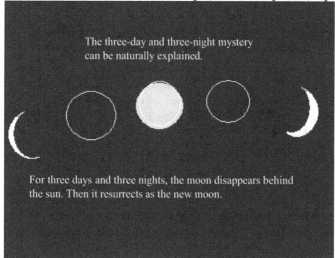

Jesus said to his disciples in Luke 24:46, "*Thus it is written*, that the Christ should suffer, and rise again from the dead the third day." In 1 Corinthians 15:4–5, it reads, "Christ died for our sins *according to the scriptures*; and that he was buried; and that he hath been raised on the third day *according to the scriptures*." ***Thus it is written "and according to scriptures."*** **However, no Old Testament scriptures** can be found to verify this claim.

Fig. 18-5. Three days n nights explained.

Yet another religious symbol falls into question as an astronomical misunderstanding. The ancients never could explain where the moon went for three days and three nights after the old moon. It simply disappeared near the sun, and then it resurrected in the western sky after sunset. You could say it sits on the right-hand side of the sun at new moon. Jonah spent three days and nights in the whale. Jesus resurrects after three days and nights.

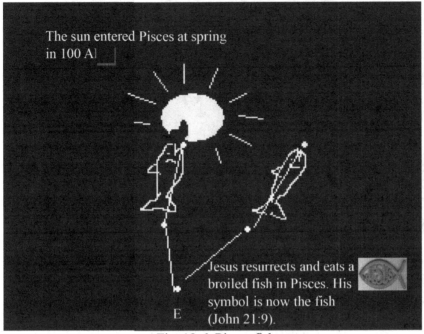

The sun entered Pisces at spring in 100 A]

Matthew 4:19

And Jesus said to them, "Follow me, for I will make you fishers of men." Other versions say, "Follow me, and I will make you fish for people."

Jesus resurrects and eats a broiled fish in Pisces. His symbol is now the fish (John 21:9).

E

Fig. 18-6. Pisces fish

What is the first thing Jesus does after the resurrection? He eats a broiled fish. Why? Now the sun was in Pisces, and the fish is its symbol.

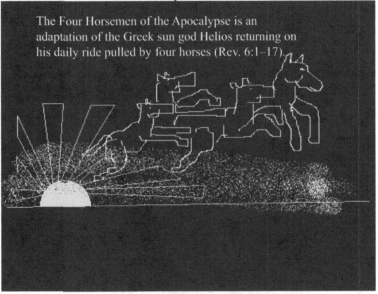

The Four Horsemen of the Apocalypse is an adaptation of the Greek sun god Helios returning on his daily ride pulled by four horses (Rev. 6:1–17).

Fig. 18-7. Helios arising

The Revelation story of the Four Horsemen of the Apocalypse is yet another rendition of the ancient Greek sun god Helios being pulled by the same team. The return of Jesus and the resurrection is a misunderstanding of the sun's annual movement and its movement along the zodiac.

ig. 18-8. If the sun could speak.

Almost all of the prophetic biblical sayings of Jesus can interchange the name "Jesus" with the word "nature," and they still make sense. The sun is the source of everything on this planet. The sun is coming quickly, and the sun is the Alpha and the Omega, the beginning and the end, the first and the last, the truth, the light and the life.

The resurrection - is it an astronomical misunderstanding of the suns annual movement?

Fig. 18-9. The resurrection.

Chapter 19

Sun Gods and Moon Gods through the Ages

Fig. 19-1. The many sun gods worldwide.

Our ancient ancestors worshipped all kinds of astronomical misconceptions. They worshipped the Pleiades, they faced the sun at dawn, and they celebrated the summer solstice at Stonehenge, as it is a solar alignment tool for the sun's rising on June 21 and setting on December 21. There are probably other astronomical uses it was made for. The most ancient astronomical depiction seems to be a 40,000 BC lunar association with a pregnant woman at Venus of Laussel or Lasceaux. The Greeks thought Helios was a sun god pulled by four horses. The Sphinx might have some association with Leo the Lion, or was it a cherub with a lion symbol? Mithras is an ancient Indian concept of the sacred Bull of Heaven being killed. Mithraism crept westward across Persia, and Roman soldiers embraced it. Sol Invicta was the invincible sun that the Romans also worshipped. The Egyptians worshipped the sun god Ra. They thought the rays of the sun would bring wisdom to the Pharaoh. Sun-related worship was prevalent throughout human history. Who can forget the Aztecs sacrificing thousands of humans to the sun? Who can forget El Dorado, the sun god of the Amazon, and the treasures that were spent trying to find its elusive city of pure gold?

Fig. 19-2. Pulling out a beating heart.   Fig. 19-3. Offering the heart to the sun.

The Aztecs who lived where Mexico City is located today once practiced sun worship, which involved removing a still-beating heart from a living human being and offering it to the sun. Cortez, leader of the conquistadors who subdued the Aztecs, had witnessed this. It has also been confirmed that the Aztecs ate the bodies of the sacrificed humans. While this may seem barbaric, Christians participate in communion every Sunday and ceremoniously drink the blood and eat the body of Christ in great willingness and devotion.

Fig. 19-4. The Incan sun pillar.   Fig. 19-5. Kinich Ahau, Mayan sun god.

The Incans who lived at Machu Picchu carved this sun pillar from the bedrock. They watched the sunrise/sunset motions of the sun during the year and created a very reliable calendar by using this pillar. On the right, the Mayans had a sun god named Kinich Ahau.

Fig. 19-6. Hirohito, the sun emperor.

Even as late as the 1940s, Japanese people considered their emperor to be the living sun. They were not allowed to look at him. The rising sun is shown on the flag of Japan. Notice all of the sun motifs that the emperor wore on his apparel and his hat.

Fig. 19-7. Buddha at dawn.

The Buddha received enlightenment under a bodhi tree just before sunrise. He saw a star shining brightly before the sun rose. The idea that a star and the sun are involved in this story reinforces the hypothesis that misunderstanding astronomy led to worldwide inventing of supernatural ideas. Buddhism still follows a lunar calendar, so the moon connection remains.

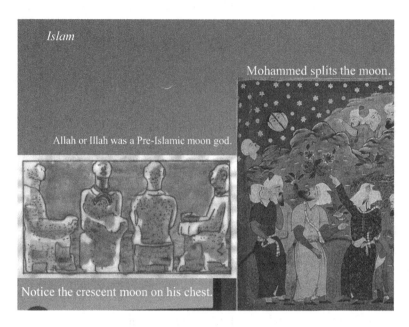

Fig. 19-8. Islam and the moon.

Pre-Islam has an ancient connection with moon worship. Allah was worshipped as a moon god long before the time of Mohammed. Clay figures (left) have been unearthed that show worshippers with crescent moon shapes upon them. Quran 54:1–2 and (painting above right) shows Mohammed splitting the moon, which is scientifically inaccurate. Islam today follows a lunar calendar. The imams go outside and look for the new moon when they begin their rituals. The Islamic flag has a crescent moon upon it and so do most of the mosques.

Fig. 19-9. Surya   Fig. 19-10. Surya's solar halo

On the left is an ancient Hindu sculpture showing Surya, the sun god. He has flames on his arms and wheel-like shapes. Hindus facing the east at sunrise frequently worshipped Surya. (That's the sun they are worshipping.) On Fig. 19-10, notice the yellow halo around Surya's head, the wheels, and the many horses pulling his chariot. It's somewhat similar to Helios.

148

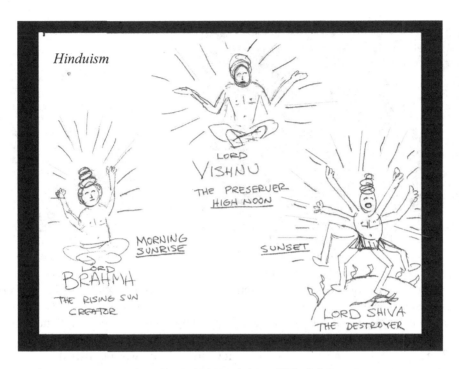

Fig. 19-11. Solar origins of Hinduism.

Hinduism has a solar origin in its gods. Brahma is the rising sun or the creator of the day. Vishnu is the noontime sun or the preserver of the day. Lord Shiva is the destroyer of the day, the setting sun, and his many arms are likened to the fingers of a setting sun. Many Hindu gods are also affiliated with the planets. Hindu temples are aligned to the east and the rising sun.

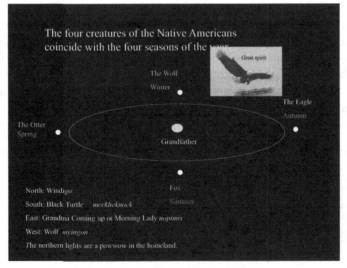

Fig. 19-12. Native four corners.

Even the Native Americans have four creatures, the otter, the wolf, the fox, and the eagle, to associate with the four seasons of the year. Notice the sun was called Grandfather.

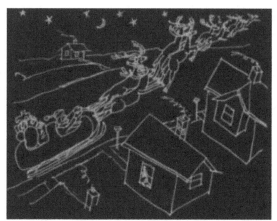

Fig. 19-13. Santa's ride   Fig. 19-14. Saint Nicholas.

Santa Claus is yet another adaptation of sun worship that arose from the AD 1000 Norse story of Woden, or Odin. He supposedly rode across the sky on an eight-legged reindeer named Sleipnir. He probably was a misinterpretation of Mercury, which moves quickly and is near to the sun. The merging of English stories of Father Christmas along with Christian stories of Saint Nicholas and Odin combined into a new version. The Dutch immigrants to America brought Sinterklaas. In 1773, the American press came out with a book on St. A. Claus. In 1823, *The Night Before Christmas* by Clement Clarke Moore was published, and Santa Claus was pulled across the sky on a chariot with eight reindeer. It merged Helios or Apollo elements into this new episode. Thomas Nast made a red-suited painting of St. Nick famous in 1870. He has all of the motifs of the sun. He wears a red suit, and a team of quadrupeds pulls him across the sky. He gives gifts greatly, just like the sun does.

Of course, the story is playful and harmless, but it is a good example of how far an original story can be twisted into a different version. What started as Ra is reinterpreted as Helios becomes Apollo pulled by a team of horses to Sol Invicta to Christ to Odin to Claus. This is precisely the problem that occurred to many mythologies. They evolved the personification of a human form from what is a natural thing. Humans are guilty of personifying so much of nature. (She's blowing a gale.) Even God is a personification of nature. He is of the weather, space, and the heavens. The North American version of Santa Claus further developed in the nineteenth and twentieth century from the English Father Christmas and the historic figure named Saint Nicholas.[1] He lived in Myra (now Demre), Turkey, in the fourth century. This image of him (above right) is from a medieval church in Bulgaria.

Fig. 19-15. Fighter jets and radar escort the modern-day Santa Claus.

———

[18] https://en.wikipedia.org/wiki/Santa_Claus

150

Does Praying Up Really Makes Sense?

Fig. 19-16 Jesus praying up   Fig. 19-17 Hands praying up

Almost every religion prays upward. This is yet another astronomical misconception. We modern humans have been to the moon and back and have not seen anything up there that would answer our prayers.

When an astronaut goes for an untethered spacewalk, he or she is most likely not praying up but instead praying down to be back safely in his or her spacecraft or safely back down on the Planet Earth. As one can see, there is nothing between the ground and vacant space. These old myths about the realm up above us being the place where God resides are derived from ancient misnomers and misunderstandings of weather and astronomy. As science provides us with factual explanations and understandings of these realms, it will cause humans to question their beliefs and then to adjust current practices.

Fig. 19-18.
There is nothing up there except vacant space.

Chapter 20

The Dark Side of the Christian Religion

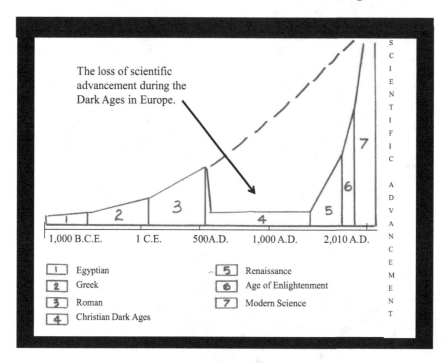

The loss of scientific advancement during the Dark Ages in Europe.

1,000 B.C.E.	1 C.E.	500A.D.	1,000 A.D.	2,010 A.D.

SCIENTIFIC ADVANCEMENT

1 Egyptian
2 Greek
3 Roman
4 Christian Dark Ages
5 Renaissance
6 Age of Enlightenment
7 Modern Science

Fig. 20-1. Dark Ages slump

One of the problems with embracing alternative cosmologies such as religion as a cosmological model is that it encourages superstition and not a rational understanding of the natural world. What happened during the height of Christendom in the world has long been known as the Dark Ages, a time of church-dominated society, a total embracing of superstition, and a lack of scientific advancement that led to a decline in the overall advancement of civilization in the fields of medicine, astronomy, engineering, and mathematics. Plagues, influenzas, wheat fungus infections, and lack of sanitation were amongst the problems they were troubled with. While religion does have the potential to do real good, like uniting people and giving people something to believe in, it also has the potential to be very manipulative, such as controlling what will be talked about, what will be accepted, and what is official doctrine. Whenever humans stifle information, alter information, or refuse to listen to another point of view, they are setting themselves up for some negative consequences.

What happened to Galileo in 1633 is a mild example of the church nearly squelching the pursuit of knowledge and condemning an innocent man while other so-called heretics were sentenced to death. Galileo attempted to get the Catholic Church to listen to his astronomical theories, but they denied him and thus sentenced him to house arrest for the remainder of his life. It wasn't until 1823 that the church acknowledged his heliocentric theory. It was not until 1992 that Pope John Paul II asked for forgiveness of the wrongs done to Galileo.

Fig. 20-2. Book burning.

Book burning and destruction of pagan sites was used extensively in religious fervor by destroying those works deemed heretical. Many religions worldwide did this kind of activity. Christianity practiced it throughout the Dark Ages. By destroying books and free thought, it was hoped to bring an end to disbelievers. The end result was only stifling things temporarily. Many great historical works were lost in such madness. If an almighty deity were so omnipotent, then why would God require destruction of anything so harmless as information? (Unless that deity was really not very powerful.) Even capitalizing the word "God" is manipulative and controlling.

Men and women were burned alive for possessing a Bible during the Dark Ages. It was illegal for non clergy to have a Bible or to quote scripture.

Fig. 20-3. Burning people alive.

What follows is a list of Christian atrocities by Christians courtesy of Vlassis G. Rassias from his book *Demolish Them!* They are listings of recorded book burnings and pagan temple site destruction over the ages.

314 .D. Denouncement of goddess Artemis worship at Council of Ancyra and Christian Church attacks non-Christians.

324 A.D. Constantine declares Christianity official religion of the Roman empire. Oracle of the god Apollo destroyed by him and he tortures the Pagan priests to death. Non Christians evicted from Mount Athos and local Hellenic temples destroyed.

326 A.D. Constantine, following the instructions of his mother Helen, destroys the temple of the god Asclepius in Aigeai of Cilicia and many temples of the goddess Aphrodite in Jerusalem, Aphaca, Mambre, Phœnicia, Baalbek, etc.

330 Constantine steals the treasures and statues of the Pagan temples of Greece to decorate Nova Roma (Constantinople), the new capital of his Empire.

335 Constantine sacks many Pagan temples of Minor Asia and Palestine and orders the execution by crucifixion of "all magicians and soothsayers". Martyrdom of the neoplatonist philosopher Sopatrus.

341 Flavius Julius Constantius persecutes "all the soothsayers and the Hellenists". Many gentile Hellenes are either imprisoned or executed.

346 New large scale persecutions against non-Christian peoples in Constantinople. Banishment of the famous orator Libanius accused as a "magician".

353 An edict of Constantius orders the death penalty for all kind of worship through sacrifices and "idols".

354 A new edict orders the closing of all the Pagan temples. Some of them are profaned and turned into brothels or gambling rooms. Executions of Pagan priests.

354 A new edict of Constantius orders the destruction of the Pagan temples and the execution of all "idolaters". First burning of libraries in various cities of the empire. The first lime factories are being organised next to the closed Pagan temples. A major part of the holy architecture of the Pagans turns to lime.
357 Constantius outlaws all methods of divination (astrology not excluded).

359 In Skythopolis, Syria, the Christians organise the first death camps for the torture and executions of the arrested non-Christians from all around the empire.

361 to 363 Religious tolerance and restoration of the Pagan cults declared in Constantinople (11th December 361) by the Pagan emperor Flavius Claudius Julianus.

363 Assassination of Julianus (26th June).

364 Emperor Flavius Jovianus orders the burning of the Library of Antioch.

154

364 An Imperial edict (11th September) orders the death penalty for all those that worship their ancestral gods or practice divination ("sileat omnibus perpetuo divinandi curiositas"). Three different edicts (4th February, 9th September, 23rd December) order the confiscation of all properties of the Pagan temples and the death penalty for participation in Pagan rituals, even private ones.

365 An Imperial edict (17th November) forbids the gentile (Pagan) officers of the army to command Christian soldiers.

370 Valens orders a tremendous persecution of non-Christian peoples in all the Eastern Empire. In Antioch, among many other non-Christians, the ex-governor Fidustius and the priests Hilarius and Patricius are executed. Tons of books are burnt in the squares of the cities of the Eastern Empire. All the friends of Julianus are persecuted (Orebasius, Sallustius, Pegasius etc.), the philosopher Simonides is burned alive and the philosopher Maximus is decapitated.

372 Valens orders the governor of Minor Asia to exterminate all the Hellenes and all documents of their wisdom.

373 New prohibition of all divination methods. The term "Pagan" (pagani, villagers, equivalent to the modern insult, "peasants") is introduced by the Christians to demean non-believers.

375 The temple of god Asclepius in Epidaurus, Greece, is closed down by the Christians.

380 On 27th February, Christianism becomes the exclusive religion of the Roman empire by an edict of the emperor Flavius Theodosius the Great (379-395 AD), requiring that:

All the various nations which are subject to our clemency and moderation should continue in the profession of that religion which was delivered to the Romans by the divine Apostle Peter.

The non-Christians are called "loathsome, heretics, stupid and blind". In another edict, Theodosius calls "insane" those that do not believe to the Christian God and outlaws all disagreements with the Church dogmas. Ambrosius, bishop of Milan, starts destroying all the Pagan temples of his area. The Christian priests lead the hungry mob against the temple of goddess Demeter in Eleusis and try to lynch the hierophants Nestorius and Priskus. The 95 years old hierophant Nestorius ends the Eleusinian Mysteries and announces the predominance of mental darkness over the human race.

381 On 2nd May, Theodosius deprives of all their rights the Christians that return back to the Pagan religion. In all the Eastern Empire the Pagan temples and Libraries are looted or burned down. On 21st December, Theodosius outlaws even simple visits to the temples of the Hellenes. In Constantinople, the temple of goddess Aphrodite is turned to a brothel and the temples of Sun and Artemis to stables.

382 "Hellelujah" ("Glory to Yahweh") is imposed in the Christian mass.

384 Theodosius orders the Praetorian Prefect Maternus Cynegius, a dedicated Christian, to cooperate with the local bishops and destroy the temples of the Pagans in Northern Greece and Minor Asia.

385 to 388 Maternus Cynegius, encouraged by his fanatic wife, and bishop "Saint" Marcellus with his gangs scour the countryside and sack and destroy hundreds of Hellenic temples, shrines and altars. Among others they destroy the temple of Edessa, the Cabeireion of Imbros, the temple of Zeus in Apamea, the temple of Apollo in Dydima and all the temples of Palmyra. Thousands of innocent Pagans from all sides of the empire suffer martyrdom in the notorious death camps of Skythopolis.

386 Theodosius outlaws (16th June) the care of the sacked Pagan temples.

388 Theodosius ordered to be burnt Porphyry's (c232-c300 AD) Treatise against the Christians.

388 Public talks on religious subjects are outlawed by Theodosius. The old orator Libanius sends his famous epistle "Pro Templis" to Theodosius with the hope that the few remaining Hellenic temples will be respected and spared.

389 to 390 All non-Christian date-methods are outlawed. Hordes of fanatic hermits from the desert flood the cities of the Middle East and Egypt and destroy statues, altars, libraries and Pagan temples, and lynch the Pagans. Theophilus, Patriarch of Alexandria, starts heavy persecutions against non-Christian peoples, turns the temple of Dionysos into a Christian church, burns down the Mithraeum of the city, destroys the temple of Zeus and burlesques the Pagan priests before they are killed by stoning. The Christian mob profanes the cult images.

391 On 24th February, a new edict of Theodosius prohibits not only visits to Pagan temples but also looking at the vandalised statues. New heavy persecutions all around the empire. In Alexandria, Egypt, Pagans, led by the philosopher Olympius, revolt and after some street fights they lock themselves inside the fortified temple of god Serapis (the Serapeion). After a violent siege, the Christians take over the building, demolish it, burn its famous library and profane the cult images.

392 On 8th November, Theodosius outlaws all the non-Christian rituals and names them "superstitions of the gentiles" (gentilicia superstitio). New full scale persecutions against Pagans. The Mysteries of Samothrace are ended and the priests slaughtered. In Cyprus the local bishop "Saint" Epiphanius and "Saint" Tychon destroy almost all the temples of the island and exterminate thousands of non-Christians. The local Mysteries of goddess Aphrodite are ended. Theodosius's edict declares: "the ones that won't obey pater Epiphanius have no right

to keep living in that island". The Pagans revolt against the emperor and the Church in Petra, Aeropolis, Rafia, Gaza, Baalbek and other cities of the Middle East.

393 The Pythian Games, the Aktia Games and the Olympic Games are outlawed as part of the Hellenic "idolatry". The Christians sack the temples of Olympia.

395 Two new edicts (22nd July and 7th August) cause new persecutions against Pagans. Rufinus, the eunuch Prime Minister of emperor Flavius Arcadius directs the hordes of the baptised Goths (led by Alaric) to the country of the Hellenes. Encouraged by Christian monks the barbarians sack and burn many cities (Dion, Delphi, Megara, Corinth, Pheneos, Argos, Nemea, Lycosoura, Sparta, Messene, Phigaleia, Olympia, etc.), slaughter or enslave innumerable gentile Hellenes and burn down all the temples. Among others, they burn down the Eleusinian Sanctuary and burn alive all its priests (including the hierophant of Mithras Hilarius).

396 On 7th December, a new edict by Arcadius orders that Paganism be treated as high treason. Imprisonment of the few remaining Pagan priests and hierophants.

397 "Demolish them!". Flavius Arcadius orders all the still standing Pagan temples to be demolished.

398 The Fourth Church Council of Carthage prohibits to everybody, including to the Christian bishops, the study of the books of the Pagans. Porphyrius, bishop of Gaza, demolishes almost all the Pagan temples of his city (except 9 of them that remain active).

399 With a new edict (13th July) Flavius Arcadius orders all the still standing Pagan temples, mainly in the countryside, to be immediately demolished.

400 Bishop Nicetas destroys the Oracle of the god Dionysus in Vesai and baptises all the non-Christians of this area.

401 The Christian mob of Carthage lynches non-Christians and destroys temples and "idols". In Gaza too, the local bishop "Saint" Porphyrius sends his followers to lynch Pagans and to demolish the remaining 9 still active temples of the city. The 15th Council of Chalkedon orders all the Christians that still keep good relations with their gentile relatives to be excommunicated (even after their death).

405 John Chrysostom sends hordes of gray dressed monks armed with clubs and iron bars to destroy the "idols" in all the cities of Palestine.

406 John Chrysostom collects funds from rich Christian women to financially support the demolition of the Hellenic temples. In Ephessus he orders the destruction of the famous temple of goddess Artemis. In Salamis, Cyprus, "Saints" Epiphanius and Eutychius continue the persecutions of the Pagans and the total destruction of their temples and sanctuaries.

407 A new edict outlaws once more all the non-Christian acts of worship
408 The emperor of the Western Empire, Honorius, and the emperor of the Eastern Empire, Arcadius, order together all the sculptures of the Pagan temples to be either destroyed or to be taken away. Private ownership of Pagan sculpture is also outlawed. The local bishops lead new heavy persecutions against the Pagans and new book burning. The judges that have pity for the Pagans are also persecuted. "Saint" Augustine massacres hundreds of protesting Pagans in Calama, Algeria.

409 Another edict orders all methods of divination including astrology to be punished by death.

415 In Alexandria, Egypt, the Christian mob, urged by the bishop Cyrillus, attacks a few days before the Judaeo-Christian Pascha (Easter) and cuts to pieces the famous and beautiful philosopher Hypatia. The pieces of her body, carried around by the Christian mob through the streets of Alexandria, are finally burned together with her books in a place called Cynaron. On 30th August, new persecutions start against all the Pagan priests of North Africa who end their lives either crucified or burned alive.

416 The inquisitor Hypatius, alias "The Sword of God", exterminates the last Pagans of Bithynia. In Constantinople (7th December) all non-Christian army officers, public employees and judges are dismissed.

423 Emperor Theodosius II declares (8th June) that the religion of the Pagans is nothing more than "demon worship" and orders all those who persist in practicing it to be punished by imprisonment and torture.

429 The temple of goddess Athena (Parthenon) on the Acropolis of Athens is sacked. The Athenian Pagans are persecuted.

435 On 14th November, a new edict by Theodosius II orders the death penalty for all "heretics" and Pagans of the empire. Only Judaism is considered a legal non-Christian religion.

438 Theodosius II issues an new edict (31st January) against the Pagans, incriminating their "idolatry" as the reason of a recent plague!

440 to 450 The Christians demolish all the monuments, altars and temples of Athens, Olympia, and other Greek cities.

448 Theodosius II orders all non-Christian books to be burned. All copies of Julian's work which could be found were destroyed, and they would have been lost entirely if bishop Cyril of Alexandria (376-444 AD), had not cited extracts from the first three of seven of Julian's books in his refutation of him, while admitting that he would not cite some of his srguments!

450 All the temples of Aphrodisias (the City of the Goddess Aphrodite) are demolished and all its libraries burned down. The city is renamed Stavroupolis (City of the Cross).

451 New edict by Theodosius II (4th November) emphasises that "idolatry" is punished by death.

457 to 491 Sporadic persecutions against the Pagans of the Eastern Empire. Among others, the physician Jacobus and the philosopher Gessius are executed. Severianus, Herestios, Zosimus, Isidorus and others are tortured and imprisoned. The proselytiser Conon and his followers exterminate the last non-Christians of Imbros Island, Norheast Aegean Sea. The last worshippers of Lavranius Zeus are exterminated in Cyprus.

482 to 488 The majority of the Pagans of Minor Asia are exterminated after a desperate revolt against the emperor and the Church.

486 More "underground" Pagan priests are discovered, arrested, burlesqued, tortured and executed in Alexandria, Egypt.

515 Baptism becomes obligatory even for those that already say they are Christians. The emperor of Constantinople, Anastasius, orders the massacre of the Pagans in the Arabian city Zoara and the demolition of the temple of local god Theandrites.

528 Emperor Jutprada (Justinianus) outlaws the "alternative" Olympian Games of Antioch. He also orders the execution—by fire, crucifixion, tearing to pieces by wild beasts or cutting to pieces by iron nails—of all who practice "sorcery, divination, magic or idolatry" and prohibits all teachings by the Pagans ("the ones suffering from the blasphemous insanity of the Hellenes").

529 Justinianus outlaws the Athenian Philosophical Academy and has its property confiscated.

532 The inquisitor Ioannis Asiacus, a fanatic monk, leads a crusade against the Pagans of Minor Asia.

542 Justinianus allows the inquisitor Ioannis Asiacus to convert the Pagans of Phrygia, Caria and Lydia, Minor Asia. Within 35 years of this crusade, 99 churches and 12 monasteries are built on the sites of demolished Pagan temples.

546 Hundreds of Pagans are put to death in Constantinople by the inquisitor Ioannis Asiacus.

556 Justinianus orders the notorious inquisitor Amantius to go to Antioch, to find, arrest, torture and exterminate the last non-Christians of the city and burn all the private libraries down.

562 Mass arrests, burlesquing, tortures, imprisonments and executions of gentile Hellenes in Athens, Antioch, Palmyra and Constantinople.

578 to 582 The Christians torture and crucify gentile Hellenes all around the Eastern Empire, and exterminate the last non-Christians of Heliopolis (Baalbek).

580 The Christian inquisitors attack a secret temple of Zeus in Antioch. The priest commits suicide, but the rest of the Pagans are arrested. All the prisoners, the Vice Governor Anatolius included, are tortured and sent to Constantinople to face trial. Sentenced to death they are thrown to the lions. The wild animals being unwilling to tear them to pieces, they end up crucified. Their dead bodies are dragged in the streets by the Christian mob and afterwards thrown unburied in the dump.

583 New persecutions against the gentile Hellenes by the Mauricius.

590 In all the Eastern Empire the Christian accusers "discover" Pagan conspiracies. New storm of torture and executions.

692 The "Penthekto" Council of Constantinople prohibits the remains of Calends, Brumalia, Anthesteria, and other Pagan/Dionysian celebrations.

804 The gentile Hellenes of Mesa Mani (Cape Tainaron, Lakonia, Greece) resist successfully the attempt of Tarasius, Patriarch of Constantinople, to convert them to Christianity.

950 to 988 Violent conversion of the last gentile Hellenes of Laconia by the Armenian "Saint" Nikon.[2]

---

[2] Source: Vlasis Rassias, Demolish Them!... published in Greek, Athens 1994, Diipetes Editions, ISBN 960-85311-3-6. Any similar material will be received gratefully.

Fig. 20-4 The Huss burning

John Huss was a Czechoslovakian preacher burned alive in 1415 because he did not approve of the church edict ordering the burning of the books of Wycliffe. The following are more book burning and temple site destructions. Why would pagan sites have to be destroyed if God was so powerful?

Perhaps some of the most tragic destruction by Christians of pagan sites was done to the Aztecs, Mayans, and Incans by the conquistadors. The priests destroyed many scripts. An attempt was made to annihilate every trace of their religion and their understandings of the cosmos. The Catholic Church tore down their temples and typically built a cathedral right over the top of the same site, much the same as Constantine tore down the temples to Apollo and Mars and built St. Peter's right over the top of them.

And that was only the first 1,000 years. In the year 1570, nearly all of the Mayan scripts were ordered burned by the Catholic Church. In 1600, Giordano Bruno was burned alive for embracing the sun centered theory and saying the sun was at the center of the solar system. In 1615 the books of Bruno, Copernicus and Galileo were banned by the Catholic Church.

Galileo was placed under house arrest in 1633 for saying the sun was at the center of the solar system. How could the Almighty not know those things? In Genesis 1, it says God created everything. He should have allowed this kind of revelation, but instead the church policy was to silence those who did not believe that Earth was at the center of the solar system. It causes one to wonder if the Almighty isn't a human fabrication. The real heart of the problem was that Galileo challenged scripture by saying that Earth does move and does go around the sun. The Bible reads in Ecclesiastes 1:5, "The sun rises and the sun goes down, and hastens to the place where it rises." In Joshua 10:12, it reads, "Sun, stand thou still at Gibeon, and thou Moon in the valley of Aijalon." Worst yet, a few passages later, it says this lasted for a whole day. Didn't God know that, by saying this, he was acknowledging he did not know that Earth turned? The Catholic Church had to stand beside scripture, lest their entire position crumble because, if one scriptural passage could be proven wrong, then how many more would follow? The real problem here is that, by following faith, a believer might become deluded of factual knowledge and then become intolerant and act hastefully over and above using logic, reason, and rationale. By giving credit to the unseen, the unknown delusion takes precedence over the scientific facts, we humans are susceptible to being led into very precipitous paths, and unfortunate actions might lead to long-term regrets.

Chapter 21

The Christian Religion and Destruction of the Earth?

This is the cosmological problem ...

"Now I saw a new heaven and a new earth, for the first heaven and the first earth had passed away" (Rev. 21:1).

He who comes from above is above all; he who is of the earth belongs to the earth, and of the earth he speaks; he who comes from heaven is above all.

(John 3:31).

Fig. 21-1. A new heaven and Earth

Now we arrive at the heart of the problem with accepting alternative cosmology as a cosmological model. If the model is in error of explaining the true situation we are in, then the believers of the model might be prone to making a mistake if they follow it. The biblical model demonstrates a misunderstanding of nature. It starts with Genesis 1 being a geocentric model ("In the beginning, God created the heavens and the earth"). Then in Genesis 2:17, all of knowledge becomes a sin in the garden of Eden. Man is the villain, he is sinful, nature is to be subdued, and God nearly destroys man. Knowledge (nature and science) is the evil force in biblical thinking.

In Genesis 1:28, it says, "Be fruitful and multiply and fill the earth and subdue it." Subduing nature can be a very destructive act. When Abraham nearly killed his son Isaac but killed a ram instead (Gen.22:13), it was a symbol of the sun being in Aries. Then Isaac's son Jacob was likened to the sun (Genesis 49) with his twelve children being the twelve zodiacal signs. Jesus was also likened to the sun. He is like a sun god with his twelve signs following him around. These ancient misunderstandings of the cosmos bring us to question the validity of religion other than to control people and make them follow theoretical constructs.

John 8:23 says, "You are from below, I am from above; you are of this world, I am not of this world." This clearly is a separation from this planet. While Christianity does not say "destroy this world," it does insinuate an apocalyptic way of replacing Earth. John 15:18 reads,

"If the world hates you, be aware that it hated me before it hated you. If you belonged to the world, the world would love you as its own. Because you do not belong to the world, but I have chosen you out of the world, therefore the world hates you." This verse is a mental barrier to embracing and learning natural science and acknowledges we are not from this planet, this world we call Earth. John 3:31 also informs us that he who comes from heaven is superior to he who comes from Earth. So where is heaven? It is only an idea. As Joseph Campbell said, "There is no physical heaven anywhere in the universe."[3]

Revelations 21:1 says something that is undertoned throughout the Bible, a new Earth will follow the destruction of the first. In Revelation 22:1, it says, "Behold, I come quickly." It has been two thousand years since that was written. Isn't it obvious that it isn't going to happen? It is a blatant misunderstanding of nature. To even suggest the destruction of this world, in order to believe that God or any deity will then save its inhabitants with a replacement Earth is irresponsible. This idea is totally absurd, as there is no backup planet anywhere that we can go to. We live on a small lifeboat of a planet that is immersed in a sea of death. Space is death to us. It has nothing to provide to us and will kill humans. We must take care of this planet. It is the only refuge we have. Those who think otherwise should reexamine the evidence. Up above us, space is not heaven. It is no paradise. It is 450 degrees below zero, and it is an absolute vacuum.

Those who encourage an apocalypse do not fully understand our situation and need to be reeducated regarding it. For this reason, the Bible should be placed into the same book section as *Gilgamesh*, *Jack in the Beanstalk*, *The Iliad*, The *Odyssey*, *The Sagas*, *Paul Bunyan*, *Hansel and Gretel*, and *Alice in Wonderland*. Evidence suggests that there will not be a second coming of Jesus, nor will an Islamic Madhi army return from a well to save mankind because those are ancient misunderstandings of the changing seasons, of which people long ago could not explain because they did not have science. They thought it was because of Persephone, Ceres, or Adonis going down to the underworld and rising from the ground like a blooming flower that brings spring's warmth. Those ancient misnomers are fairy tales of long ago.

Fig. 21-2. End of the world rally.   Fig. 21-3. Harold Camping.

On May 21, 2011, Harold Camping, prophetic head of the Church of God, forewarned the coming apocalyptic end of the world. Nothing happened on that date, though thousands of people worldwide prepared to leave this world at the rapture. This happened again on December 21, 2012, with the supposed end of the world via the Mayan calendar. It was utter

_____

[3] Joseph Campbell, The Power of Myth, New York, 1988 p. 56

nonsense. This kind of religious terrorism should be taken very seriously. People literally believe ancient misnomers that were said in the Bible. It could someday be used with very detrimental results if the wrong groups get a hold of weapons of mass destruction. It also costs the system a great deal of downtime, fear, stress, and loss of productivity. It is an antiquated philosophy that is very hostile to our tiny Planet Earth. Currently, Earth is the only place that can sustain life, and we have no other place to go other than via artificial means like living in the city bus-sized International Space Station and having provisions sent up from the real heaven below, Earth.

Let this be a wakeup call. Matthew 11:25 reads, "Jesus said, I thank you Father, Lord of Heaven and Earth, because you have hidden these things from the wise and intelligent and have revealed them to infants." This says that knowledge, including learning science along with astronomy, is futile as infants know more. Then it goes on to say, "All things have been handed over to me by my Father, and no one knows the Son except the Father, and no one knows the Father except the Son and anyone to whom the Son chooses to reveal him." This is condemning learning and saying that only following this one belief will be tolerated. It can be a death sentence to anybody outside of the faith if it falls into the wrong hands.

> Religion never taught us the following. Science was learned from the defiance of people who died trying to teach us scientific truth.

Fig. 21-4.

Over the millennia of biblical wisdom, there was never any mention about the Almighty God ever knowing anything about the next set of truths. The biblical writers, nor the source of the information in the Bible, knew astronomical information. So how could they have written about it?

Turn the next page, and see information that no religion ever taught or no God in all of human history ever told us. This was learned from scientists (who are educated human beings) and their personal self-sacrifice.

Chapter 22

What Science, Not Religion, Taught Us about the Heavens

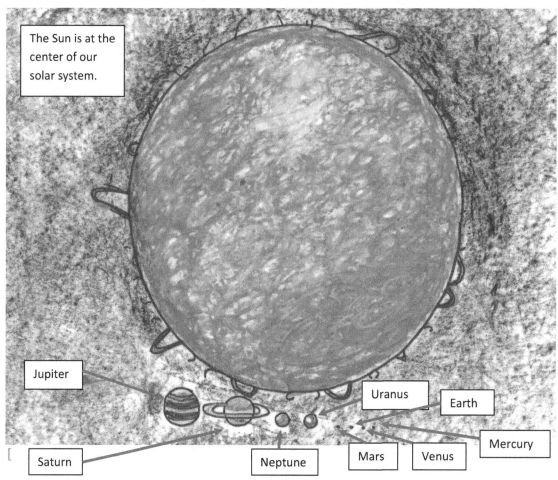

Fig. 22-1. The scale of the sun.

The sun is huge. It is nearly a million miles wide. It is four times wider than the Earth-to-moon distance. You cannot fit the sun between Earth and the moon. It is that big. You can see how small our planet Earth is by following the arrow to that tiny dot. We human beings have such terrific egos that we think our imaginary heroes have powers way beyond those of nature. But we are so wrong. The sun makes up 99 percent of the mass of the solar system. Its energy output is shocking. It puts out 383 billion trillion kilowatts per second. Every second, the sun puts out more energy than all of humanity will or has ever used.[4]

---

[4] http://www.physics.fsu.edu/courses/spring98/ast1002/sun/
http://www.telescope.org/nuffield/pas/planets/planet6.html

Fig. 22-2. The sun compared to other stars.

The sun is big when compared to Earth, but it is tiny in comparison to much larger stars.

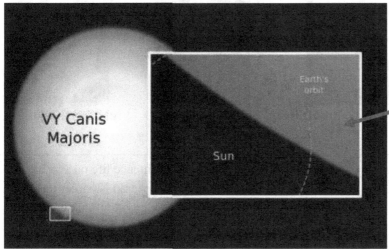

Fig. 22-3. How tiny the sun is compared to VY Canis Majoris.
The four royal Persian stars are very far away from Planet Earth.

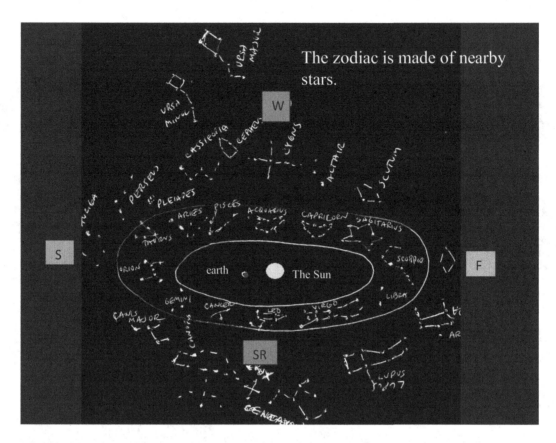

Fig. 22-4. The sun and the distribution of stars around it.

The four royal Persian stars are located 90 degrees apart from each other and distributed along the ecliptic. They are all many light-years away from us, and in actuality, they play no part in occurrences on Earth.

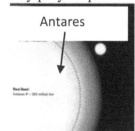
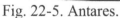
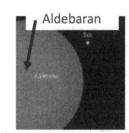

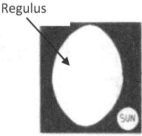

Fig. 22-5. Antares. Fig. 22-6. Aldebaran. Fig. 22-7. Fomalhaut. Fig. 22-8. Regulus.

The four royal Persian stars are very far away from us and do not influence life on Earth. Antares is a type M1 Red Giant at six hundred light-years away. Aldebaran is cooler than the sun, a K5 star at sixty-five light-years. Fomalhaut does have a planet around it that has been seen with large telescopes. It is twenty-five light-years away and a hot A3 star. Regulus, a very hot B7 star, does one rotation in 15.9 hours and is therefore oblate. It is 350 times more luminous than the sun, and it is 77 light years away.

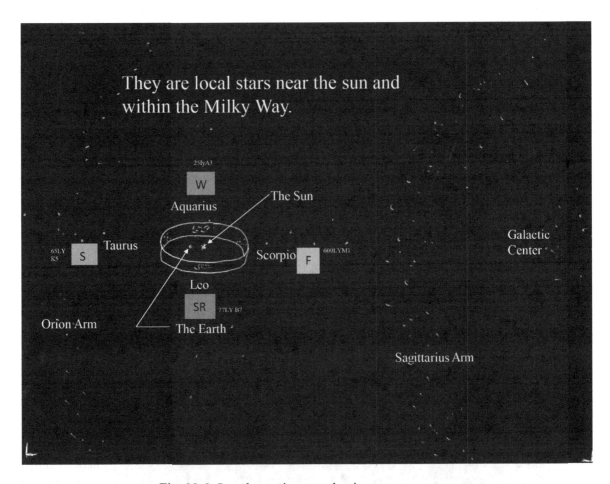

Fig. 22-9. Local stars in our galactic arm.

The ring seen here gives an idea of the zodiac. The sun is in the middle. As we move farther away from it, we get an approximate idea of where the nearby stars are located. For instance, Antares (F) is classified as an M1 red star in Scorpio, about six hundred light-years away, and it is located in the direction of the galactic center. The light-green S is the star Aldebaran, a K1 star located sixty-five light-years away in Taurus, the direction of the outer arm of our galaxy. Fomalhaut (W) is an A3 at twenty-five light-years away. Regulus (SR) is a hot B star at about seventy-seven light-years away.

Once again, the four royal Persian stars have no impact upon us humans on Earth. So why does the church place so much emphasis upon them? They put them at the center of St. Peter's Basilica in the Vatican, and they are on nearly every Catholic Church around the world. The Matthew, Mark, Luke, and John symbols have something to do with the four royal Persian stars. Why is so much importance placed upon them when they have no impact upon us? It is because of ancient astronomical misunderstandings of the cosmos. More so, it is because of a misunderstanding of nature.

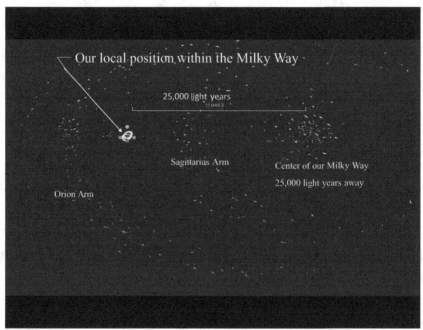

Fig. 22-10. Where we are in the galaxy.

Our local position in the Milky Way is shown. The galaxy is about one hundred thousand light-years across. Our sun is located twenty-five thousand light-years away from the center. The Sagittarius arm is in the direction of the galactic center, while the Orion arm is away from the center. Fig. 22-11 below shows 700 planets discovered around stars.

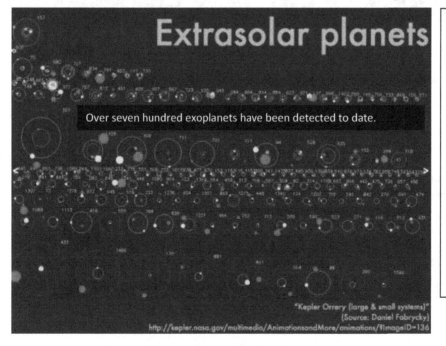

There are other planets around other stars. Space telescopes like Kepler, Spitzer, and Hubble have now discovered over seven hundred exoplanets around other stars. A few may be like Earth. In the adjacent illustration, see the dark dots of possible planets around these relatively near stars.

Fig. 22-11.

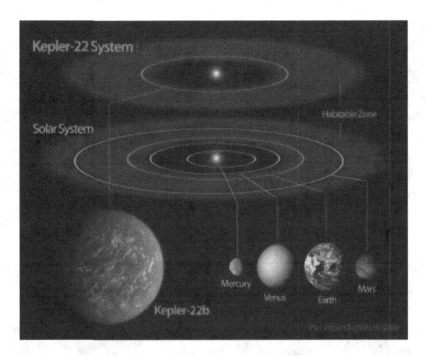

Fig. 22-12 Habitable areas

Habitable zones around stars are shown in the green. Planets around other stars have habitable zones where life might be more likely to exist. The habitable zone for hot stars would be very far from it. The habitable zone for cooler stars would be much nearer to the star. There might be exceptions, as life can adapt in remarkable ways

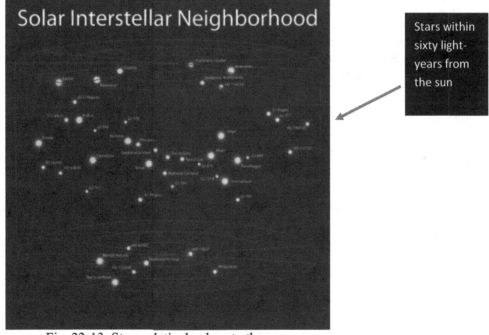

Stars within sixty light-years from the sun

Fig. 22-13. Stars relatively close to the sun.

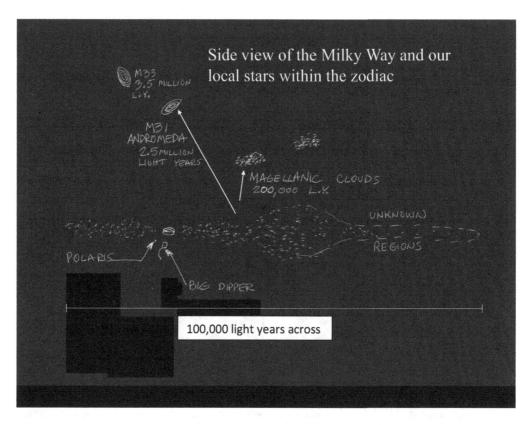

Fig. 22-14. A side view of the Milky Way.

As we zoom farther away from the Milky Way, we can see our location of local stars, and the zodiac is that tiny ring just above the Big Dipper. The Milky Way has a wheel-like shape with the hub of the wheel being the center. Nearby galaxies are illustrated, but they are much farther away than the drawing implies.

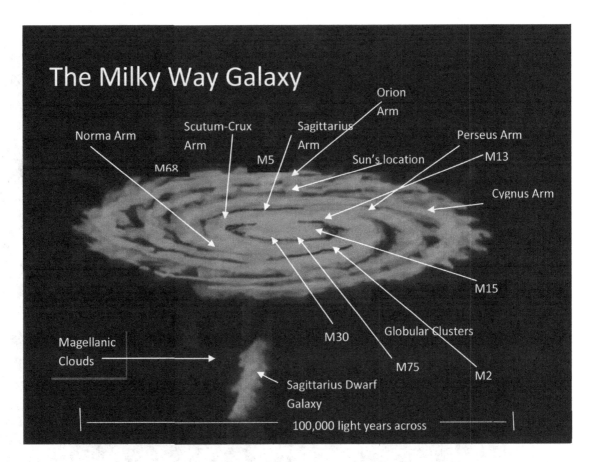

Fig. 22-15. The Milky Way.

Moving out to about two hundred thousand light-years away from the Milky Way, we can see its overall shape. It is considered to be a loosely arranged barred spiral, and our sun is located about halfway or two-thirds between the center and outer arms. Areas of the Milky Way are on the other side of the central region, of which we have no knowledge what is over there, nor do we know what is beyond the Milky Way in that direction because the core is so dense with stars that block our view.

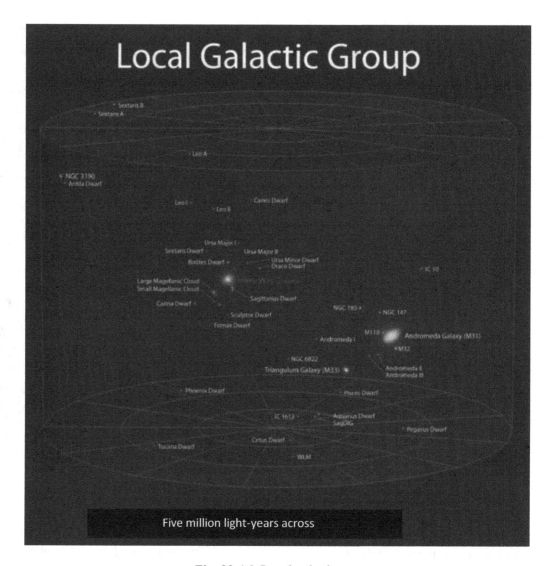

Fig. 22-16. Local galaxies.

About ten nearby galaxies are close to the Milky Way. Some are dwarf galaxies. Others like the Magellanic Clouds are companions to the Milky Way. Larger galaxies like Andromeda lay 2.5 million light-years away. The Triangulum Galaxy is about three million light-years away.

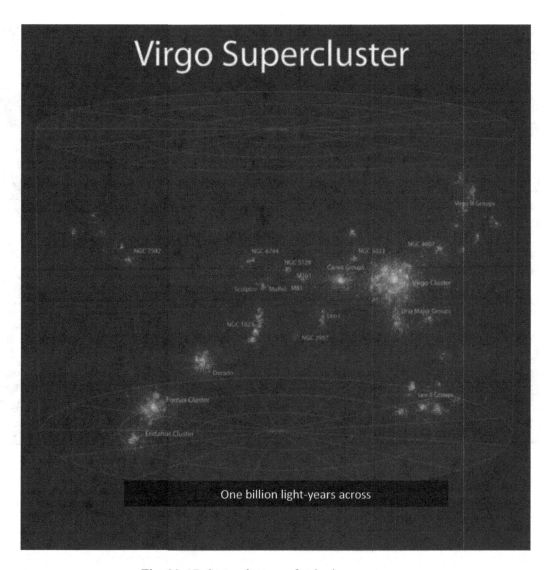

Fig. 22-17. Superclusters of galaxies.

As we move out farther, we see the nearby galaxies are a small corner of a larger grouping of galaxies. Even though the Virgo Cluster lies eighty million light-years away, our galaxy is a part of this huge conglomerate.

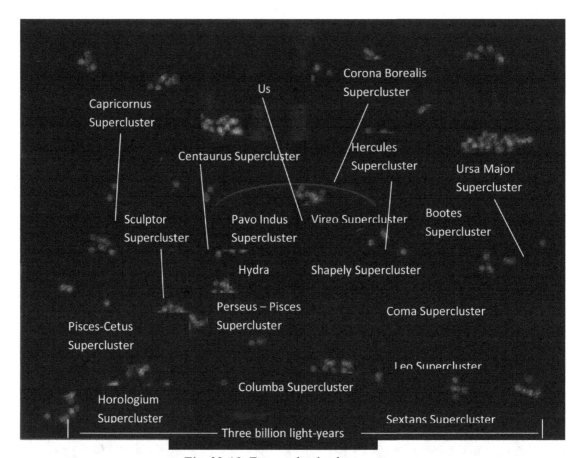

Fig. 22-18. Extra galactic clusters.

When we look at the galaxy clusters that are within three billion light-years, we can see entire long chains of galaxies extending away from us in all directions.

Fig. 22-19. The Hubble deep space view.

The Hubble Space Telescope took this very long exposure of deep space. It was in an area of the sky equivalent to Roosevelt's head on a dime held at arm's length. Underneath that area, hundreds of galaxies exist. The latest information reveals that there are 125 billion other galaxies in the universe. To ever believe that we are the only selected galaxy, within which is the only selected star called the Sun, which is orbited by the only selected planet and we are selected in the likeness of any God, is absurd. There are probably hundreds of other habitable worlds around hundreds of other stars within our galaxy alone. In all of the universe, there may very well be innumerable varieties of beings out there in all shapes and operating under very different bioprocesses than we are. The problem is that everything is so far away that we may never truly know about them.

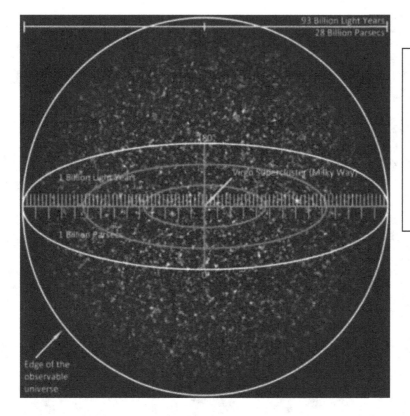

There are at least 125 billion galaxies and large numbers of galaxy clusters distributed throughout the universe.

Fig. 22-20. The edge of the universe.

We arrive at the idea of an immense universe that is rapidly expanding away from us. Every galaxy except the Andromeda Galaxy appears to be moving away. This rapid expansion of space is an important challenge to try to comprehend, and only further research and scientific study will reveal its mysteries.

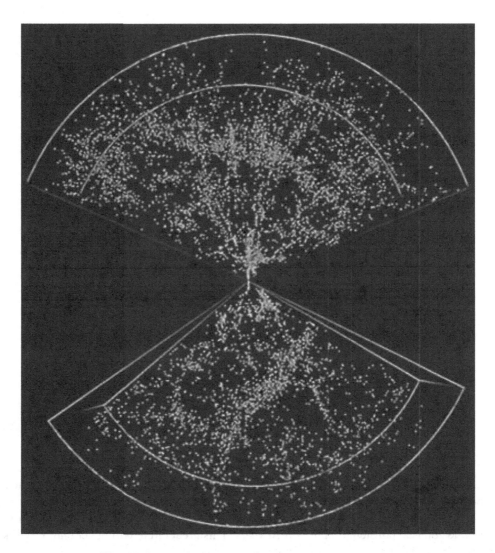

Fig. 22-21. An immense universe.

The universe is estimated to be about 13.7 billion years old. Each of these dots is a cluster of galaxies. The farthest galaxy to be seen is about 13.3 light-years away from us. It was created only a few million years after the big bang. The outermost regions of our universe still retain a temperature of two degrees above absolute zero, the distant remnant heat left over from that event that happened so long ago.

The most distant observation in the universe is 13.7 billion light-years away. It took that long for the light or energy to get here. Due to the expansion of the universe, it is now doubled that distance in size. This makes the known universe twice as far away as we know and twice as large across.

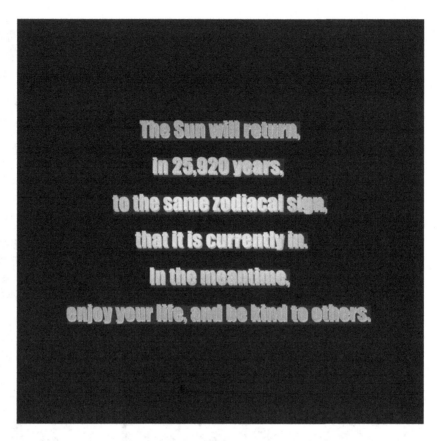

Fig. 22-22. The precessional cycle takes 25,920 years.

Now that we can see how the ancients personified the sun, we can also see how they expect the sun to resurrect to a position that it was in long ago. In fact, the sun will go full circle around the zodiac. It will pass through all twelve signs of the zodiac and again return to the same zodiacal constellation in 25,920 years. This great circle will never end. It will keep reoccurring as long as the sun is shining.

The second coming is a misunderstanding of the sun's movement.

Fig. 22-23. Jesus second coming.

Chapter 23
Bizarre Concoctions and Misinterpretations of Precession

Astrology is a prediction of outcomes based on the position of the sun along the zodiac. By using the birth sign of an individual, astrologers claim they can foresee good or bad fortune. Using the position of the sun, moon, and the planets, fortune-tellers claim they can foretell what will occur. This is pure bunk because those celestial bodies are too far away from us to cause effects.

In calculating the duration of the different yugas, there are a few differences between the Puranas. The Brahmanda Purana (1.2, 29. 31-34) specifically states that Krita or Saty-yuga is 1.44 million human years in length. Treta-yuga is 1.08 million years.

Treta Yuga1: 1.08 million solar years	72 + 36=108	1.5 zodiac movement
Satya Yuga: 1.44 million solar years	72 + 72 = 144	2 zodiacal signs moving
Krita Yuga: 172,8000 solar years	144 X 12 = 1,728	3/4 of 1 zodiacal sign
Treta Yuga: 1296000 solar years	2,160 X 6 = 12,960 (half of zodiac cycle)	
Kali Yuga: 432,000 solar years	432 is 6 degrees of sun's movement	
Dvapara Yuga: 864,000 solar years	864 is a movement of 12 degrees	

72, 144, 432, 864, 1,728, 2,160, and 12,960 have to do with the 25,920 solar cycle.

From the Bhagavhad Gita 8:17, "Virtue, wisdom, and religion characterize the cycle of Satya. Being no ignorance and vice, the yuga cycle lasts 1.728 million years. The Treta Yuga is introduced and lasts 1.296 million years. In the Dravapan cycle, there is an even greater decline in virtue and religion vice increasing, and this yuga lasts 864,000 years. And finally in Kali Yuga, the cycle we are currently in, lasting five thousand years (The Bull), there is an abundance of strife, ignorance, irreligion, and vice. True virtue is practically nonexistent, and this yuga lasts 432,000 years. "

Fig. 23-1. An example of misunderstandings of precession used in religion.

Ancient cultures did have some notions about the movement of the sun around the zodiac. They did the math and tried to explain it, but they never had enough information. They did not have science. In India, these numbers were incorporated into the Hindu religion. They knew the sun moved a degree every 72 years (Treta Yuga). The number 72 is how many years it takes for the sun to shift one degree to the west. If one multiplies 72 x 1.5 =108, that would be one and half degrees of movement. 72 x 2 = 144 is two degrees of movement. That number is used as the Satya Yuga and also mentioned in Revelation 7:4. Next is the number is 432, which is 72 x 6 degrees of movement. In Hinduism, every 432,000 years, Brahma returns from the cosmic ocean. The number of 1,728 years is equal to 24 degrees of the sun's movement. Finally, if one multiplies 72 by 360 degrees, the answer is 25,920 years. This is the complete 360 degree movement of the sun around the zodiac. Because the ancients could not make scientific sense of any of the sun's movement, they took those numbers and incorporated them into religious ceremonies.

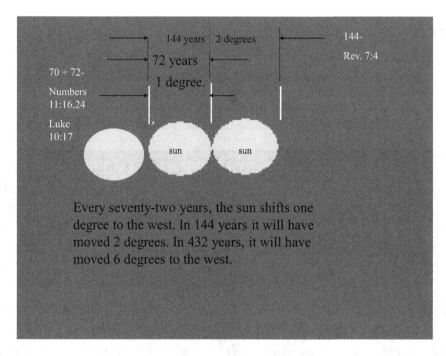

Fig. 23-2.   72 years equals one degree of westward movement of the sun.

Osiris had seventy-two accomplices to his murder. Islam incorporated the seventy-two virgins story from Hadith 2687, but the number is not mentioned in the Koran. In the Bible, it mentions the number seventy sixty-one times. Is it just a coincidence that Jesus had seventy-two disciples, as mentioned in Luke 10:17?

Joseph Campbell mentioned this story in his Powers of Myth interview with Bill Moyers.

"Vishnu sleeps in the cosmic ocean, and the lotus of the universe grows from his navel. On the lotus sits, Brahma, the creator. Brahma opens his eyes and a world comes into being, governed by an Indra. Brahma closes his eyes, and a world goes out of being. The life of a Brahma is 432,000 thousand years. When he dies, the lotus goes back, and another lotus is formed, and another Brahma." [5]

So the ancient Hindus knew about this number of 432. They knew it had some kind of great cosmic connection. Little did they know it really had to do with precession of the sun.

---

[5] Joseph Campbell, The Powers of Myth, New York, 1988, p. 63

The first of these beings was in the form of a lion, the second looked like an ox, the third had the face of a man, and the fourth the form of an eagle, with wings spread out as though in flight [the four royal Persian Stars]. (Rev. 4:7)

I am the A and the Z the beginning and the end of all things, I am the all powerful one, who is, and was and is coming again [the sun's continuous circuit of the zodiac]. (Rev. 1:8)

I watched as he broke the sixth seal, and there was a vast earthquake, and the sun became dark like black cloth, and the moon was blood red [a total solar eclipse and a lunar eclipse]. (Rev. 6:12)

I saw four angels standing on the four corners of the earth, (2) I saw another angel coming from the east carrying the great seal of the living God [the four royal Persian stars]. (Rev. 7)

The 12 Pearly Gates [the zodiac]. (Rev. 21:21)

144,000 [72 years x 2 = 144] (Rev. 14:1) and three 144,000 (Rev. 21:17) temple walls are 144 cubits (Rev. 7:4).

I am the bright morning star [Venus]. (Rev. 22:16)

Fig. 23-3. Bible passages that have something to do with misunderstood astronomy.

The Revelation 4:7 passage incorporates wings onto the four royal Persian stars, making them angels. Revelation 6:12 says a total solar eclipse and a total lunar eclipse occurred on the same day. That is impossible. Revelation 7 tells about four angels on the four corners of Earth. First, Earth has no corners. It is round. The four royal Persian stars do rise in the east, and they are placed where the four seasons were around 3000 BC.

The pearly gates is a nice description of the many individual signs of the zodiac (Rev. 21:21). In Revelation 7:4, 7:8, 14:1, and 21:17, these biblical passages use the zodiacal number 144. In Revelation 22:16, Jesus says he is the morning star. Compare that to Isaiah 14:12. "How you are fallen from heaven, Oh Lucifer, son of the morning!" Lucifer was a Latin word meaning "phosphorus" and was often associated with the Planet Venus. In Genesis 28:12, Jacob's ladder appears to describe the zodiac passing overhead.

The number of the beast is 666 (Rev. 13:18). 144,000 divided by 66.6 = 2,162 (Rev. 7:4). The correct number of 2,160 is one-twelfth of the sun's movement along the zodiac. Could the ancients have miscalculated 2,162 for 2,160? This is the accurate number. 2,160 x 12 = 25,920 years, the complete circle of the zodiac by the sun. This number of 2,162 x 12 = 25,944 is incorrect but is very close and curious. Was somebody trying to calculate precession?

Fig. 23-4. The number 666.

If we take the Hindu Satya Yuga period of 1,440,000 and divide it by 2,160 (the number of years for the sun to precess 30 degrees or one zodiacal constellation along the ecliptic), we come up with 666. This is the ominous number of the beast mentioned in Revelations 13:18. Is this just some coincidence or another misinterpretation of numbers from long ago that have to do with the movement of the sun along the zodiac? We may never know.

Chapter 24
Humans and the Universe

Humans and the Universe

1. We are made of the same elements as the sun: carbon, iron, magnesium, hydrogen, calcium, and vitamins A, B, C, D, and so forth.

2. We each have electric fields. We generate electricity. The Earth is surrounded by electricity and magnetism; so is the sun.

3. We eat and drink from the earth. All nourishment comes from the earth, which utilizes sunlight to grow life-forms.

4. The earth is rotating at 1000 MPH. The Earth is moving around the sun at 66,000 MPH. The sun is moving in the direction of Vega at 44,000 MPH and the galactic arm at 170,000 MPH. The Milky Way is moving through space at 310,000 MPH.

5. To see the Earth from space, we would see no borders, boundaries, or separation. All is one. Nobody comes from anywhere else. The Earth is our lifeboat.

6. Our senses are connected to the universe, giving us awareness of what it is.

7. Positive thinking can create blissful chemicals in the brain.

8. In truth, there is no separation. We are one with the universe.

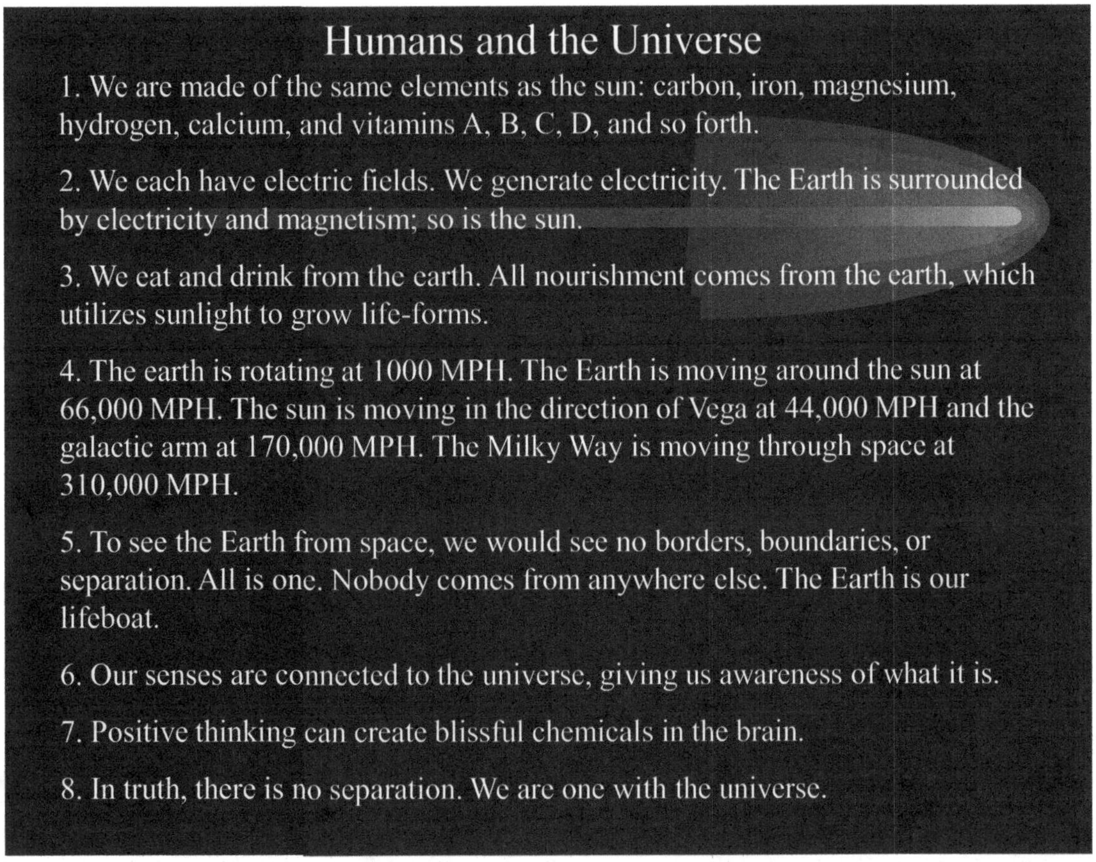

Fig. 24-1. We are in motion.

We are a part of the universe. We are made of the materials of the universe, and we are moving along with it, but we have no actual plugged-in connection to it. Tranquility, randomness, and chaos are capable throughout the universe. Understanding nature is one of the best recipes for living in harmony with nature. Nature could not care less if we get in its way. It is up to us to foresee and predict outcomes based upon our knowledge of natural forces.

Astrology is using celestial bodies such as the sun, moon, planets, stars, and zodiac to predict outcomes of good or bad fortune.

Luke 21:25 – "There will be signs in the sun, and the moon, and stars, and on the earth distress of nations confused by the roaring of the sea and the waves. People will faint from fear and foreboding of what is coming upon the world, for the powers of the heavens will be shaken. Then they will see the Son of Man coming in a cloud with power and great glory. Now when these things begin to take place, stand up and raise your heads, because your redemption is drawing near. "

Chapter 25

It Is Up to You to Decide

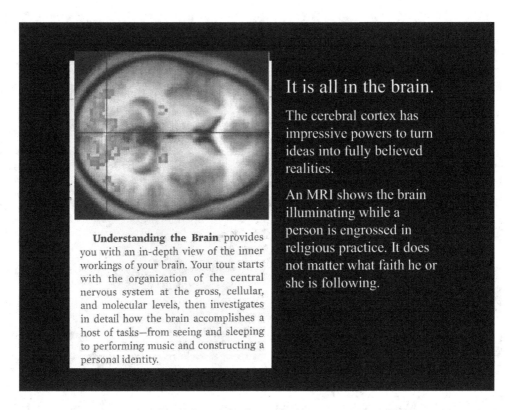

It is all in the brain.

The cerebral cortex has impressive powers to turn ideas into fully believed realities.

An MRI shows the brain illuminating while a person is engrossed in religious practice. It does not matter what faith he or she is following.

Understanding the Brain provides you with an in-depth view of the inner workings of your brain. Your tour starts with the organization of the central nervous system at the gross, cellular, and molecular levels, then investigates in detail how the brain accomplishes a host of tasks—from seeing and sleeping to performing music and constructing a personal identity.

Fig. 25-1. A brain scan.

It is all in your brain. It is up to you to decide. With enough information, the final analysis is based on how much you understand. The brain understands reality via the five senses. It also understands reality by dreams and inner thoughts, but are they real? Reality might seem to come from having dream, reading a book, or having a psychotic experience. The problem is deciphering what is real. The only standard to decide what is real is by using the five senses—sight, smell, hearing, tasting, and touch. If it passes those five tests, then it can be deemed real. When a MRI brain scanner is hooked up to a patient, whether he or she is Christian, Muslim, or Jew, the brain has been shown to illuminate when certain stimuli are shown. Similar areas of the brain are illuminated when a monk, shaman, priest, believer, mediator, guru, or atheist philosopher engages in his or her practice.[6] This would mean it is a universal characteristic of humans, no matter what faith they follow, to have sensations of heightened awareness whenever they think of whatever they believe.

---

[6] , http://en.wikipedia.org/wiki/File:FMRI.jpg

Conclusion

Human beings noticed the four royal Persian stars prior to five thousand years ago. They are located in the four positions that the sun was at during spring, summer, fall, and winter. Ancient man noticed the sun's annual movements, and this started as a very natural observation, one that was very useful to tell what time of year it was. However, as time went on, it was rapidly pulled into religious and supernatural misunderstandings. It was personified, as humans so readily do, into an imaginary hero, incorporated into many mythologies, and drawn right into the heart of the major religions of today. We take for granted that most people do not care nor comprehend what they are worshipping. They do it because it feels good, it is a social activity, and it seems right. They follow a ritual that was passed down to them, even though they or their leaders may not know the origins of why they do what they do. But this is the great quandary. If humans do not understand what they believe, then they can be easily misled down a very irrational and potentially destructive path, even causing notions about the destruction of human life on Planet Earth. Abstract and unprovable ideas about heaven or a paradise being a realm up above us are entirely unfounded. The only true heaven is that which is experienced by everyday life on the Planet Earth. It is far better for humanity to realize the truth by understanding nature and using logic, evidence, scientific facts, and the scrutiny of reason, no matter how unfulfilling or unsatisfying they may be, then to mislead others into the realm of superstition and delusion.

When children ask you, "What is up there?" what will you tell them? Will you tell them the truth?

Let children look through a telescope! Learning about astronomy can teach children the truth. They will better understand the celestial objects by seeing them, and it will help them make rational sense of the universe. Children are our greatest hope for survival of our species.

Real Evidence of the Sun versus the Son

	Jesus	The sun
1. Do we know when this was created?	6 BC to AD 4?	Five billion years ago
2. Do we know how it was created?	Immaculate conception?	Condensing hydrogen
3. Can we see it physically?	No	Yes
4. Can we test or falsify the evidence/miracles?	No	Yes
5. Is there a physical description?	No	Yes
6. How does it work?	Unknown medium, a miracle	Thermonuclear fusion
7. How does the energy transfer?	Unknown/prayer perhaps?	Radiation, light, and energy
8. What amount is energy output?	Unknown, except belief	383 billion trillion kw per/sec
9. What dimensions can you give?	A large group of believers	865,000 miles across
10. Does it bring light to the world?	Not physically but spiritually	Yes, it does!
11. Does it provide life to the world?	A spiritual life	Yes, everything's reliant on the sun
12. Does spiritual mean it is real?	Hearsay, Jesus is a real spirit	No, spiritual is subjective
13. Can you readily demonstrate this power?	Via miracles	Yes, via solar energy, a sunburn, the use of a magnifying glass, a heat wave, the northern lights, and fusion
14. Are the miracles provable?	Not always	The sun is reliable, always shining
15. How long will this last?	Until the end of the age?	Another five billion years
16. Can you prove its existence?	Gospels and unconfirmed reports	Look at it and go blind*
17. If its light went out what would happen?	Very little	Catastrophic to all of life on earth
18. Add up all the falsifiable truths.	0	17

Falsifiable means it can be verified and tested with physical evidence, a confirmation of material demonstrated with scientific method and corroborated from all sources as being factual.

*Never look at the sun, you will go blind. It took millions of years of sunlight to grow biomass and then millions more to biodegrade it and make oil and gas. Even our cars are totally reliant on the sun.

Bibliography References

Page 1 - [1] (p.17), Zend Avesta Sirozah 13
[1] Chapter 2, verse Bundahishn
Page 2 -[3] *The History of Ancient Astronomy* p.13, 130, 480 and 481
[4]Origine de Tous les Cultes "These stars (Aldeberan, Regulus, Antares and Fomalhaut) received the pompous denomination of royal stars."
(p.257-259)
[5] ibid 529-530.
[6] Popular Astronomy in April 1945 (Ch. 2, verse 7 on page 152).
[7] Popular Astronomy in April 1945 (p.155)
8Popular Astronomy in April 1945 (p.156)
[9] American Peoples Encylopedia
Page 3 [10] Robert Burnham Jr. p.1057, 1486, 1658, 1807.
Page 5 -[11] The Book of John video by Snorri Gudmundsson.
Page 7 - [12] Science, August 2007

14, 15,19,20,21,22,114   Stellarium

16. Harding, Arthur, Astronomy page 252

17. en.wikipedia.org/wiki/File:Taurus_IAU.SVg   image of Taurus   zodiac – signs.gif

18. space.today.org/SolSys/Earth/OldStarCharts.html   and wwe.real – dream – catchers.com/...interpreting_the_ojibwe_pictograph...

24. -[13] www.mt.net, the zodiac, cherubims and the sphinx   the hiddenlighthouse.blogspot.com

27. – The artblog.org A Visit to the British Museu   Winter   ɔells Power of Myth p.98   right-American Peoples
Encyclopedia Vo.2 p. 514

28. Harding, Arthur, Astronomy, page 255

29. [1] The Zodiac of Dendera. www.lindahall.org   saturnaincosmology.org/files/denderah

30. [1] The Zodiac of Dendera. www.lindahall.org   ishtartsgate.com/phpBB3/viewtopic.php?f=31&t=1656
Bibliography

32. American Peoples Encylopedia Vol. 2. P.195. A Sun God   indofiles.org   and the sun god is –
historyhuntersinternational.org/wp-content/gallery/helios/

33, 34. www.biblewalks.com.sites.lowerGalilee info is from members.bib-arch.org

34. prophetess.lstc.edu/~rklein/documents/faithHef.htm

35. astrology.about.com

37. Abrahams journey –http://www.hope.edu/

38. www.ucalgary.ca/~elsegal/shoke/MHCSo2_mosaicMusings.html

38. Bibleplace.com and lower enlargement is – lajupaulk3blogspot.com

39. www.maxhead.org/pol/showthread.php?&tid=426772&t...760   lajupaulk3.blogspot.com

40. www.theoi.com/GalleryZ4html.

44. catholic_resources.org/Photos?RAVEENA.htm

45. Wikipedia Raveena, Italy

46. Google Chartes Cathedral

47. Top-Sharonsscrapbook.blogspo   Molten Sea - ejmmm2007.blogspot.com.   lower-templemount.org

48. enwikipedia.org/wiki/battle_of_the_milvianBridge

49. www.eyeoutof thegarden.com/2011/10/immormon_not_christian.html

50. The Vatican and St.Peters

51. Miraclerosarymission.org

52. www.tombes-sepultures.com/crbst_144.html

53. www.miraclerosarymission.org/stpetertour.html   mcah.columbia.edu

54. mcah.columbia.edu

55. news.discovery.com.historyNews

56-60. enwikipedia.org/wiki/st_peter's_basilica   . panoramicearth.blogspot.com/…st.peters-basilica-rome-papal-altar.ht

61.. enwikipedia.org/wiki/Irenaeus

62.. Saintpetersbasilica.org/statues/StPeter/StPeter.html

63. enwikipedia.org/wikimars_   esotericonline.net

64. sacred-destinations.com

66. Wiki Veronica   g8ors.blogspot.com

70. blogtravelpod.com/travel – photo/skyisblu/9/…close…/+pod.htmlPAUL

73. sintpetersbasilica.org/floorplan.htm

74. staticearth.net/distance.htm

75. staff.knox.edu/fmcandre/cosmology.html

76. thinkprogress.org/…/its-anti-flat-earth.day-conservapedia-theory-of-r…

78. The World's Last Mysteries by Readers Digest

81. saintpetersbasilica.org/Interior/Dome?Dome.htm

82. saintpetersbasilica.org/

83. saintpetersbasilica.org/Interior/Dome?Dome.htm

84. www.myspace.com/johnpaulthegreat   lower left- www.ourcatholicprayers.com/blessed-sacraments.html   right-enwikipedia.org/wiki/monstrance

85. Crownedplaces.canalblog.com

86. Information courtesy of Thomas Hedin

87. luxuryistanbultours.com

89. the-hagia-sophia.landmarks.com.uk/hagia-sophia-plan   bottom image- hagiasophia.com/160_years_old_secret.php

90. http://en.wikipedia.org/wiki/File:Jesus-Christ-from-Hagia-Sophia.jpg golden Jesus with crux behind him

91. utopianidealists.yuku.com   smarthistory.khanacademy.org

94. Duluth News Tribune article   www.2012spiritual.info/the-mystery-of-the-gothic-cathedrals.html   Hercules.gcsu.edu/~rviav/chartes.html
The Christ Conspiracy by Achraya p. 173

96. www.artandarchitecture.org.uk/images/conway/23987b11.html

97. Harzan.blog.163.com/.../10046502006833115672

98. Rams of Egypt Wikipedia

102. Mithraism Wikipedia

103. Harding, Arthur, Astronomy. P. 277

104. forum.prisonplanet.com>...>Genuinephilosophydiscussion

107. Scientific American December 2009. p.77

108. Harding, Arthur, Astonomy p.253

109. www.bibliotecapleyades.net

111. Scientific American December 2009

112, 113.. enwikipedia.org/wk/biblical_Magi

114-118. enwikipedia.org/wiki/file:Journey_of_the_Magi.jpg

124, 125, 126 Google saros patterns

131. Maps of Israel. www.es.flinders.edu.au   The Childhood of Jesus ebibleteacher.com   Map from Zondervan Bible

133. the 12apostles.tsmj.org   Wiki maps of the Decapolis

140. http://en.wikipedia.org/wiki/File:Khashkhamer_seal_moon_worship.jpg Sin the moon god

142. Joseph Campbell mentions in his book Powers of Myth on page 179, starting with "Definitely. The say so themselves.."

145. Sun Lore of All Ages by William Tyler Olcott 1914

146. PBS Machu Picchu

147. PBS The Life of the Buddha   . www.warhistory.ie/world - war-2/emperor-hirohito.-1901-09.htm

148. en.wikipedia,org Quran 54:1-2 www.jesus-is-saviour.com/False%20Religions/.../moon_god.htm   sury image –
users.hartwick.edu/hartleyc/surya.htm

150. www.physorg.com/news/2010-12-santa-claus-et-physicist.html   Saint Nick – enwikipedia.org and Santa Claus

151. www.askwhy.co.uk/christianity/0780Bookburning.php   Jesus praying up: grannysuesnews.blogspot.com

  Hands praying up: mynuggestsoftruth.blogspot.com   Uranus-dionysis praying up; arlingtonrenewal.org NASA STS41-B 984

152. Nobellife.com

153. Google Constantine

154-157. Vlasis Rassias, Demolish Them!... published in Greek, Athens 1994, Diipetes Editions, ISBN 960-85311-3-6. Any similar material will be
received gratefully.

154. Heritic Burned alive- vindication.xanga.com/505737249/item/

158. Wikipedia.org/wiki/file:Jan_Hus_at_the_Stakejpg

159. NASA

160. sketches by EN
162. theheckdoitknow.blogspot.com   [1] http://www.physics.fsu.edu/courses/spring98/ast1002/sun/

163. our sun and canis major – rozenek.com

163,165,166. Atlasoftheuniverse.com

165. motherboardvice.com

167. Google The Milky Way aintitcoll.com

169. jesuspictures – photos.blogspot.com

172, 173, 174. 175,NASA

175. scoopit.com
180. Google MRI research and Brain Activity http://www.dailymail.co.uk/sciencetech/article-1339517/God-brain-Scans-activity-religious-
people-meditate.html   http://www.pewforum.org/Science-and-Bioethics/How-Our-Brains-are-Wired-for-
Belief.aspxhttp://www.scientificamerican.com/article.cfm?id=belief-in-the-
brainhttp://www.plosone.org/article/info%3Adoi%2F10.1371%2Fjournal.pone.0007272

Other books used as reference ;

365 Starry Nights by Raymo

Fingerprints of the Gods, by Graham Hancock

The Sun in the Church by Heilbron

The Transformations of Myth Through Time by Joseph Campbell

The Power of Myth by Joseph Campbell

The Christ Conspiracy – The Greatest Story Ever Sold by Acharya S.

The Book Your Church Doesn't Want You To Read by Tim C. Leedom

The Universe Fifth Edition by Kaufmann Freedman

A Demon Haunted World by Carl Sagan

Discoveries and Opinions of Galileo by Stillman Drake

The Egyptian Book of the Dead by E.A. Wallis Budge

The Constellations - An Enthusiasts Guide to the Night Sky by Lloyd Motz and Carol Nathanson

Photo Credits.

Page #   Source

1.   Fig. 1-1 Artwork by Eric Norland

2.   Fig. 1-2, Fig. 1-3, Fig. 1-4 sketch by EN

3. Fig. 1-5 EN sketch

4. Fig. 1-6 EN sketch

5. Fig. 1-7 http://en.wikipedia.org/wiki/File:FMRI.jpg the brain under an MRI

6. Fig. 1-8, Fig. 1-9 EN

7. Fig. 1-10, Fig. 1-11 http://en.wikipedia.org/wiki/File:Views_on_Evolution.svg a graph showing the acceptance of evolution worldwide

8. Fig. 1-12 EN sketch of American Peoples Encylopedia Vol. 2,. P. 196, Archaeology

9. Fig. 1-13, Fig. 1-14 EN

10. Fig. 2-1 EN

11. Fig. 2-2, Fig. 2-3 EN

12. Fig. 2-4, Fig. 2-5 EN

13. Fig. 2-6, Fig. 2-7, Fig. 2-8 EN

14. Fig. 3-1 Stellarium

 15. Fig. 3-2, Fig. 3-3 Stellarium

16. Fig. 3-4 EN

17. Fig. 3-5, EN, Fig. 3-6 en.wikipedia.org/wiki/File:Taurus_IAU.SVg   image of Taurus

18. Fig. 3-7 by Bob King, Fig. 3-8 en.wikipedia.org/wiki/File:Orion_IAU.svg

19. Fig. 3-9 Stellarium

20. Fig. 3-10 Stellarium

21. Fig. 3-11 Stellarium

22. Fig. 3-12 Stellarium

23. Fig. 3-13 EN

24. Fig. 3-14 EN

25. Fig. 3-15 EN

26. Fig. 3-16. EN

27. Fig. 4-1 EN, Fig. 4-2 EN

28. Fig. 4-3 EN

29. Fig. 4-4 denderah by Eric Norland

30. Fig. 4-5 denderah by Eric Norland

31. Fig. 4-6 Aeon sun god by Eric Norland

32. Fig. 4-7, Helios, Fig. 4-8 Verulam EN

33. Fig. 4-9 http://en.wikipedia.org/wiki/File:ZodiacMosaicTzippori.jpg Sepphoris image of sun disc and horses.

34.Fig. 4-10 EN

35. Fig. 4-11 EN

36. Fig. 4-12EN

37. Fig. 4-13 Eric Norland

Fig.4-14http://en.wikipedia.org/File:Moln%C3%A1r_%C3%81brah%C3%A1m_kik%C3%B6lt%C3%B6z%C3%A9se_1850.jpg Abraham

38. Fig. 4-15Abraham slays Isaac EN,

39. Fig. 4-16 Tiberius EN

40. Fig. 4-17 Youthful sun god EN

41 Fig. 4-18 Bir Chana Eric Norland

42. Fig. 5-1 twinkling stars EN

43. Fig. 5-2 Four angels EN

44. Fig. 5-3 Angels EN

45. Fig. 5-4 Angels on ceiling EN

 46. Fig. 5-5 Portico Chartes Fig. 5-6 St. Michael by EN

 47. Fig. 5-7 Wheels of the zodiacEN Fig. 5-8 Molten Sea EN Eric Norland sketch Fig. 5-9 Holy of Holies EN

      48. Fig. 6-1 http://en.wikipedia.org/wiki/File:Constantine_multiple_CdM_Beistegui_233.jpg coin with Constantine and Apollo on it

49.Fig. 6-2 http://en.wikipedia.org/wiki/File:Constantine_burning_Arian_books.jpg constantine orders book burning

Fig. 6-3 http://en.wikipedia.org/wiki/File:Follis-Constantine-lyons_RIC_VI_309.jpg shows a coin with constantine and sol invicta upon it. 309 to 310 AD

50. Fig. 6-4 Sketch by Eric Norland of Neros Circus and Temple to Apollo and Mars.

51. Fig. 6-5, en.wikipedia.org/wiki/File:ChristAsSol.jpg   Fig. 6-6 Circus of Nero by EN

52. Fig. 6-7 http://en.wikipedia.org/wiki/File:Plan_of_Circus_Neronis_and_St._Peters.gif a floor plan view of Circus of Nero and St. Peters

53. Fig. 6-8 Sketch by Eric Norland of above view looking down on St. Peters.

54. Fig. 6-9 http://en.wikipedia.org/wiki/File:Basilica_di_San_Pietro_1450.jpg an old print of the old St. peters

Fig. 6-10 http://en.wikipedia.org/wiki/File:Pope-peter_pprubens.jpg a portrait of St.Peter

55. Fig. 6-11 Sketch by Eric Norland of interior of old St. Peters.

56. Fig. 6-12 Close up view of interior by Eric Norland

57. Fig. 6-13 Eric Norland photo   Fig. 6-14 http://en.wikipedia.org/wiki/File:St_Peter%27s_Square,_Vatican_City_-_April_2007.jpg   this view is looking toward the river from above St. peters and shows the sundial like shapes

58. Fig. 6-15 http://en.wikipedia.org/wiki/File:Vatican_Altar_2.jpg   this is a spanning view of the interior center of St. peters basilca.

59. Fig. 6-16   Thinkstock 101862449 view of Baldachin and 4 pendants

60. Fig. 6-17 http://en.wikipedia.org/wiki/File:Interiorvaticano8.jpg The Baldachin with St. Luke on the right. Author is Ricardo André Frantz

Fig. 6-18 is a photo taken by Nancy Norland

61. Fig. 6-19 en.wikipedia.org/wiki/Irenaeus   Fig. 6-20 http://www.pbase.com/bmcmorrow/image/115465925 Brian McMorrow image of St. Mark with the Lion   Brian McMorrow photos

62. Fig. 6-21 http://www.pbase.com/bmcmorrow/image/115465922 Brian McMorrow image of St. John with the Eagle.   Brian McMorrow photos

Fig. 6-22 http://www.pbase.com/bmcmorrow/image/115465921 Brian McMorrow image of St. Matthew with the little man.   Brian McMorrow photos

63. Fig. 6-23 http://simple.wikipedia.org/wiki/File:Interiorvaticano8.jpg this is St. Luke the Ox in St. Peters.

64. Fig. 7-1 http://en.wikipedia.org/wiki/File:Saint_Helena.jpg   St. Helen

65. Fig. 7-2 http://en.wikipedia.org/wiki/File:Saint_Longinus.jpgLonginus   and Mars; http://en.wikipedia.org/wiki/File:Mural_warrior.jpg a pompey like image of Mars

66. Fig. 7-4 http://en.wikipedia.org/wiki/File:Saint_veronica.jpg Veronica   Fig. 7-5 http://en.wikipedia.org/wiki/File:Sandro_Botticelli_La_nascita_di_Venere_-_Google_Art_Project.jpg venus by Botticelli

Fig. 7-5B Venus symbol by Eric Norland

67. Fig. 7-6 http://en.wikipedia.org/wiki/File:Zeus_pompei.JPG Jupiter from Pompei.

Fig. 7-7 http://en.wikipedia.org/wiki/File:Saint_Andreas.jpg image of St. Andrew

68. Fig. 7-8 EN   Fig. 7-9 Ancient Terra cosmos

69. Fig. 7-10 Mary on the moon. Sketch by Eric Norland

70. Fig. 7-11 Thinkstock IMAGE # 77861087 OF St. Peters dome

71.Fig. 8-1
http://www.google.com/imgres?hl=en&sa=X&tbo=d&biw=1152&bih=745&tbm=isch&tbnid=THWMRCmAgXVpxM:&imgrefurl=http://en.wikipe
dia.org/wiki/File:The_Chair_of_Saint_Peter_adjusted.JPG&docid=V9efm989gXmXCM&imgurl=http://upload.wikimedia.org/wikipedia/common
s/0/09/The_Chair_of_Saint_Peter_adjusted.JPG&w=3372&h=2700&ei=89nsUJW8DpT3qQHKmYHAAg&zoom=1&iact=rc&dur=419&sig=116699
523163848905527&page=1&tbnh=144&tbnw=190&start=0&ndsp=31&ved=1t:429,r:6,s:0,i:109&tx=110&ty=96 Chair of St. Peter in Vatican

72. Fig. 8-2 httpen.wikipedia.orgwikiFileMilky_Way_Night_Sky_Black_Rock_Desert_Nevada.jpg   credit Steve Jurvetson

73.Fig. 8-3 http://upload.wikimedia.org/wikipedia/commons/5/54/PetersdomGrundriss.jpg floor plan of new St. Peters

74. Fig. 8-4 http://commons.wikimedia.org/wiki/File:Ptolemaic_system_(PSF).png earth centered solar system

75. Fig. 8-5, 8-6 by EN

76. Fig. 8-7, 8-8 by EN

77. Fig. 8-9 EN

78. Fig. 8-10 http://en.wikipedia.org/wiki/File:Stonehenge_plan.jpg an above view of Stonehenge   Fig. 8-11 sketch by Eric Norland

79, Fig. 8-12, 8-13 by EN

80. Fig. 8-14 by EN

81. Fig. 8-15 by EN

82. Fig. 8-16 Think Stock #95069854 image of the dome of St.Peters.

83. Fig. 8-17 Thinkstock image #160311332   Fig. 8-18 by EN

84 Fig. 8-19 Sketch by Eric Norland   Fig. 8-20 by EN,   Fig. 8-21 http://en.wikipedia.org/wiki/File:Monstrans.jpg this is a red monstrance
depiction   Fig. 8-22 Think Stock # 127060172 image of a monstrance

81. saintpetersbasilica.org/Interior/Dome?Dome.htm

85. Fig. 9-1 http://en.wikipedia.org/wiki/File:Chartres.jpg this is the portico of Chartes Cathedral and the photo credit goes to Nina Aldin Thune

86. Fig. 9-2 sketch by Eric Norland Fig. 9-3 http://en.wikipedia.org/wiki/File:Coupole_Val-de-Grace_fresque_Pierre_Mignard.jpg this is a wiki
image of Val de Grace give credit to Myrabella.

87. Fig. 9-4 Eric Norland photo at Hagi Sophia Fig. 9-5 http://en.wikipedia.org/wiki/File:HagiaSophia_DomeVerticalPano_(pixinn.net).jpg view
of hagi sophia interior   Fig. 9-6 http://en.wikipedia.org/wiki/File:Hagia_Sophia_Interior_Dome.jpg scaffold and dome cleaning of Hagi Sophia.

88. Fig. 9-7 http://en.wikipedia.org/wiki/File:HagiaSophia_DomeVerticalPano_(pixinn.net).jpg view of the ceiling and dome of Hagi Sophia
museum.

89. Fig. 9-8 Image of a seraphim on the ceiling of Hagi Sophia by Nitin Bhardwaj with thanks!

90. Fig. 9-9 http://en.wikipedia.org/wiki/File:Jesus-Christ-from-Hagia-Sophia.jpg golden Jesus with crux behind him

Fig. 9-10 Eric Norland image.

91. Fig. 9-11 Eric Norland

92. Fig. 9-12 Eric Norland

93. Fig. 9-13 Holy Rosary by Eric Norland

94. Fig. 9-14 Duluth News Tribune article and Fig. 9-15 Achyraya

95. Fig. 9-16 Sketch by EN. Fig. 9-17 http://en.wikipedia.org/wiki/File:KellsFol027v4Evang.jpg from the Book of Kells, showing a tapestry with 4 symbols of the season.

96. Fig. 9-18 EN, Fig. 9-18 EN and Fig. 9-20

97. Fig. 9-21 Sketch by Eric Norland

98. Fig. 10-1 Eric Norland chart.

99. Fig. 10-2 Stellarium, Fig. 10-3 http://en.wikipedia.org/wiki/File:SFEC_EGYPT_KARNAK_2006-001.JPG rams at Karnak temple. Taken by Steve F E Cameron from Merlin England

100. Fig. 10-4 and Fig. 10-5 Eric Norland sketch of the Ten Commandments

101. Fig. 10-6 and Fig. 10-7 Eric Norland photos

102. Fig. 11-1 and Fig. 11-2 by Eric Norland

103. Fig. 11-3 Eric Norland   info from, Harding, Arthur, Astronomy. P. 277

104.Fig. 11-4 http://en.wikipedia.org/wiki/File:12_Tribes_of_Israel_Map.svg this is a map of the 12 tribes of Israel. Fig. 11-5 Eric Norland

105. Fig. 11-6   http://en.wikipedia.org/wiki/File:San_Juan_Bautista_por_Joan_de_Joanes.jpg St. John the Baptist Fig. 11-7 by Eric Norland Fig. 11-8 http://en.wikipedia.org/wiki/File:Solar_eclipse_1999_4_NR.jpg total solar eclipse photo with baily beads. Fig. 11-9 sketch by EN

106. Fig. 11-10 Photo by EN, Fig. 11-11 by EN, Fig. 11-12 Jesus fish symbol photo by EN

107. Fig. 11-13, Fig. 11-14 by EN

108. Fig. 11-15, Fig. 11-16 by EN

109. Fig. 12-1 sketch by EN, from Harding, Arthur, Astonomy p.253   Fig 12-2 http://en.wikipedia.org/wiki/File:Equinox_path.png this shows the years of the sun precessing along ecliptic

110. Fig. 12-3 http://en.wikipedia.org/wiki/File:Earth_precession.svg shows earth precessing   Fig. 12-4 http://en.wikipedia.org/wiki/File:Precession_N.gif this shows the years precessing since 0 Fig. 12-5 http://en.wikipedia.org/wiki/File:70Apostles.jpg artwork of the 70 or 72 disciples

111.Fig.12-6 http://en.wikipedia.org/wiki/File:Antikythera_model_front_panel_Mogi_Vicentini_2007.JPG Photo credit to Mogi Fig. 12-7http://en.wikipedia.org/wiki/File:NAMA_Machine_d%27Anticyth%C3%A8re_1.jpg this is a piece of the famed Anticythera machine found off in the Med. Sea and said to be lost in 80BC.

112.Fig. 13-1 EN sketch

113. Fig. 13-2 sketch by EN. enwikipedia.org/wiki/file:Journey_of_the_Magi.jpg   Fig. 3-3.EN

114.Fig. 13-4 EN sketch

115. Fig. 13-5 sketch by EN

116. Fig. 13-6 http://en.wikipedia.org/wiki/File:Journey_of_the_Magi.jpg shows the 3 wisemen riding on camels.

117. Fig. 13-7 This is the 3 wise men. http://en.wikipedia.org/wiki/File:Magi_(1).jpg credit to be given to Nina-no

118. Fig. 13-8 Sketch by EN

119. Fig. 13-9 Sketch by EN

120. Fig. 13-10 Stellarium
121. Fig. 13-11 EN, Fig. 13-12 EN
122. Fig. 13-13, Fig. 13-14 EN
123. Fig. 13-15 EN
124. Fig. 14-1 EN
125. Fig. 14-2 EN

126. Fig. 14-3 EN

127. Fig. 14-4 http://en.wikipedia.org/wiki/File:Heilige_Walburga.jpg St. Walpurgis is celebrated on May. 1st. http://en.wikipedia.org/wiki/File:Candle-calendar.jpg a candle for Candlemass Day on Feb. 2   http://en.wikipedia.org/wiki/File:All-Saints.jpg all Saints Day   http://en.wikipedia.org/wiki/File:Alexandr_Ivanov_015.jpg transfiguration painting.

128. Fig. 14-5 sketch by EN

129. Fig. 15-1 Sketch by EN

130. Fig. 15-2 Sketch by EN

131. Fig. 16-1 http://en.wikipedia.org/wiki/File:The-Decapolis-map.svg a map of Israel

132. Fig. 16-2 by EN, Fig. 16-3 by EN, Fig. 16-4 http://en.wikipedia.org/wiki/File:Po_vodam.jpg Jesus walking on water

133.Fig. 16-5 by EN, Fig. 16-6 http://en.wikipedia.org/wiki/File:First_century_palestine.gif map of jesus land

134. Fig. 16-7 by EN, Fig. 16-8 by EN

135. Fig. 17-1 http://en.wikipedia.org/wiki/File:1581_Bunting_clover_leaf_map.jpg old map with Jerusalem as center of world.

Fig. 17-2 http://en.wikipedia.org/wiki/File:First_century_palestine.gif map of jesus land

136. Fig. 17-3 by EN, Fig. 17-4 http://en.wikipedia.org/wiki/File:Alexandr_Ivanov_015.jpg transfiguration painting. http://en.wikipedia.org/wiki/File:Transfiguration_by_Lodovico_Carracci.jpg free Wiki of transfiguration.

137. Fig. 17-5, Fig. 17-6 by EN

138. Fig. 17-7, Fig. 17-8 by EN

139. Fig. 17-9, Fig. 17-10, Fig. 17-11 sketches by EN

140. Fig. 18-1 by EN, Fig. 18-2 http://en.wikipedia.org/wiki/File:Khashkhamer_seal_moon_worship.jpg Sin the moon god

141. Fig. 18 -3 http://en.wikipedia.org/wiki/File:Solar_eclipse_1999_4_NR.jpg total solar eclipse photo with baily beads

142. Fig. 18-4, Fig. 18-5 by EN

143. Fig. 18-6, Fig. 18-7 by EN

144. Fig. 18-8 by EN, Fig. 18-9 http://en.wikipedia.org/wiki/File:Der-Auferstandene_1558.jpg the resurrection

145. Fig. 19-1, http://en.wikipedia.org/wiki/File:Stonehenge2007_07_30.jpg a nice sideview of Stonehenge
http://en.wikipedia.org/wiki/File:Great_Sphinx_of_Giza_-_20080716a.jpg the Sphinx
http://en.wikipedia.org/wiki/File:Creation_of_the_Sun_and_Moon_face_detail.jpg god by Michelangelo
http://en.wikipedia.org/wiki/File:NGC_3810_(captured_by_the_Hubble_Space_Telescope).jpg a spiral galaxy

http://en.wikipedia.org/wiki/File:Musei_Vaticani_-_Mithra_-_Sol_invictus_01136.JPG mithra and sol invicta mentioned together200 to 300 AD

http://en.wikipedia.org/wiki/File:Aten_disk.jpg this is a Pharoah receiving light from the sun god Ra or Aten. Used on page 141 of book.

http://en.wikipedia.org/wiki/File:Venus-de-Laussel-vue-generale-noir.jpg venus of Laussel or LasCaux as used on page 141 of book

146. Fig. 19-2, Fig. 19-3, Fig. 19-4 PBS photos on my TV, Fig. 19-5 http://en.wikipedia.org/wiki/File:God_G_Kinich_Ahau_2.jpg kinich ahau, the Mayan sun god

147. Fig. 9-6 http://en.wikipedia.org/wiki/File:Hirohito_in_dress_uniform.jpg Hirohito

Fig. 9-7 http://en.wikipedia.org/wiki/File:Buddha_Meditating_Under_the_Bodhi_Tree,_800_C.E.jpg The Buddha sitting underneath the Bodhi Tree. Buddha tree Sketch by EN.

148. Fig. 19-8 http://en.wikipedia.org/wiki/File:Suryatanjore.jpg Surya, god of the India sun

Fig. 19-9 http://en.wikipedia.org/wiki/File:WLANL_-_23dingenvoormusea_-_Suryabeeldje.jpg sculpture of surya, the sun god

Fig. 19-10http://en.wikipedia.org/wiki/File:Mohammed_Splits_the_Moon.jpg Mohammed splitting the moon.

149. Fig. 19-11, Fig. 19-12 sketches by EN
150. Fig. 19-13 sketch by EN, Fig. 19-14, http://en.wikipedia.org/wiki/File:Nikola_from_1294.jpg Saint Nicholas Fig. 19-15;
https://www.google.com/search?as_st=y&tbm=isch&hl=en&as_q=santa+fighter+jet&as_epq=&as_oq=&as_eq=&cr=&as_sitesearch=&safe=im
ages&tbs=sur:fc&biw=1152&bih=702&sei=sMknUsS_GqGSyAHoz4CoBg#facrc=_&imgrc=tD2B0ye0_I7v1M%3A%3BqMkd_SD4hBkQ1M%3Bhttp
%253A%252F%252Fupload.wikimedia.org%252Fwikipedia%252Fcommons%252Fd%252Fd4%252FNTS_Santa_Jet_Fighter_Escort.jpg%3Bhttp%
253A%252F%252Fcommons.wikimedia.org%252Fwiki%252FFile%253ANTS_Santa_Jet_Fighter_Escort.jpg%3B549%3B378 Santa Claus and
fighter jets

151. Fig. 19-16, http://en.wikipedia.org/wiki/File:Albrecht_D%C3%BCrer_Betende_H%C3%A4nde.jpg hands praying upward by Albrecht Dure
Fig. 19-17, rhttp://en.wikipedia.org/wiki/File:Christ_in_Gethsemane.jpg Jesus praying up in the Garden of Gethsemane

Fig. 19-18, NASA STS41-B 984 NASA image of a spacewalk.

152. Fig. 20-1, Sketch by Eric Norland

153.Fig. 20-2 http://en.wikipedia.org/wiki/File:Constantine_burning_Arian_books.jpg constantine orders book burning

154. Fig. 20-3 http://en.wikipedia.org/wiki/File:Wickiana5.jpg burning 3 witches at the stake 1585   154-157 Timeline is courtesy Vlassius G.
Rassias from his book Demolish Them!

158. Fig. 20-5, http://en.wikipedia.org/wiki/File:Jan_Hus_at_the_Stake.jpg John Huss being burned at the stake

http://en.wikipedia.org/wiki/File:Spiezer_Chronik_Jan_Hus_1485.jpg John Huss burned alive

159. Fig. 21-1 Apollo 13 photo of the earth from the moon by NASA

160.Fig. 21-2, sketch by EN, Fig. 21-3 sketch by EN

162. Fig. 22-1, Scale of the solar system sketch by EN.

163. Fig. 22-2, http://en.wikipedia.org/wiki/File:Sun_and_VY_Canis_Majoris.svg our sun compared to Canis Majoris

Fig. 22-3, http://en.wikipedia.org/wiki/File:Star-sizes.jpg the size of solar system planets and the sun and stars

164. Fig. 22-4 sketch by EN, Fig. 22-5 http://en.wikipedia.org/wiki/File:Redgiants.svg Antares scale and the sun and Arcturus

Fig. 22-6 http://en.wikipedia.org/wiki/Aldebaran illustration of Aldebaran

Fig. 22-7, http://es.wikipedia.org/wiki/Archivo:Heic0821f.jpg Image of Fomalhaut

Fig. 22-8 Fig. 22-9 Regulus sketch by EN

165. Fig. 22-9 Sketch by EN

166. Fig. 22-10 by EN, Fig. 22-11-
http://www.google.com/imgres?hl=en&lr=&sa=X&tbo=d&biw=1152&bih=702&tbm=isch&tbnid=vomX13x5hBnQPM:&imgrefurl=http://waiferx
.blogspot.co this is a NASA image of possible Exoplanets

167. Fig. 22-12, http://en.wikipedia.org/wiki/File:Kepler-22b_System_Diagram.jpg habitable zones around earth and other stars

Fig. 22-13, http://en.wikipedia.org/wiki/File:3_Solar_Interstellar_Neighborhood_(ELitU).png local group of stars

168. Fig. 22-14 by EN

169. Fig. 22-15 sketch of Milky Way by EN.

170. Fig. 22-16 http://en.wikipedia.org/wiki/File:5_Local_Galactic_Group_(ELitU).png local galactic group

171. Fig. 22-17 http://en.wikipedia.org/wiki/File:6_Virgo_Supercluster_(ELitU).png supergroup of galaxies

172. Fig. 22-18 Extra Galactic Cluster sketch by EN

173. Fig. 22-19, http://en.wikipedia.org/wiki/File:Hubble_ultra_deep_field_high_rez_edit1.jpg NASA deep space image

174. Fig. 22-20, http://en.wikipedia.org/wiki/File:Observable_Universe_with_Measurements_01.png the observable universe

175 Fig. 22-21,
http://www.google.com/imgres?imgurl=http://imagine.gsfc.nasa.gov/Images/map/northsouth_lg.jpg&imgrefurl=http://imagine.gsfc.nasa.gov/
docs/features/exhibit/map_structure.html&h=450&w=412&sz=64&tbnid=X9-
dLuk_WE1ygM:&tbnh=89&tbnw=81&zoom=1&usg=__7dmAMQ09ZJbtN4FzdGe-
dGfZfAE=&docid=rMMdHlnigCRpGM&hl=en&sa=X&ei=HYnoUPCTDZHPqQGVy4BY&ved=0CDsQ9QEwAQ&dur=721 this is a NASA image of the
known universe

176. Fig. 22-22 by EN, Fig. 22-23 http://en.wikipedia.org/wiki/File:AscensionofChrist2.jpg the ascension of Jesus

177. Fig. 23-1 by EN

178. Fig. 23-2 by EN

179. Fig. 23-3 by EN

180. Fig. 23-4 by EN

181. Fig. 24-1 by EN

182. Fig. 25-1, http://en.wikipedia.org/wiki/File:FMRI.jpg the brain under an MRI

184. Sketches by EN

185. Real Evidence by EN

Index List

About the author. Eric Norland was born in 1955 in Duluth, Minnesota and raised as a devout Presbyterian boy. Sunday morning church services were a regular routine, except during the summers, until he was in his early 20's. He graduated from the University of Minnesota Duluth with a Bachelor of Fine Arts degree and also took many classes in astronomy. His favorite art history teacher was professor Thomas Hedin, who taught a class on how to read the allegories and symbols beneath the surface of renaissance paintings. At the age of 25, in 1981, Norland moved to California and lived out of his car for the next two and a half years. During that time in Santa Barbara, an exploration of faith commenced. For about 6 months on each Sunday, various churches were visited and a comparative review of the many branches of Christianity were made that opened up a big question as to why there are so many different Christian churches. It was at about this same time, in the early Reagan administration, that cold war tensions were at their highest regarding a nuclear conflict with the Soviet Union. The term 'Mutually Agreed Upon Destruction' seemed to Norland an oxymoron and a hopelessly nonnegotiable term. It was at this point, in 1983 that Norland decided to travel around the world on a bicycle named Friend. It was a hope to reach out and meet Russians and tell the rest of the world, that it is better to be friends than enemies. From 1983 through 1986, Norland traveled around the world on a bicycle and even met some Russians, shaking their hands and feeling it was all a misunderstanding. He pedaled his bike across 33 countries and began to see even more religious diversity. Variations and change could only mean one thing. The hand of man must be involved in these different religions. There had to be an explanation as to how humans came up with so many diverse religious themes. The question on Norland's mind was; what is the source, especially in the Christian religion? Where did these symbols originate? It was that question which led to the development of this book. He realized, there had to be some core reason which initially inspired mans definition of God. After many years of pondering this, and while recovering from back surgery he found inspiration from Joseph Campbell's book The Power of Myth. Campbell mentions the resurrection period of three days and nights might have something to do with the monthly disappearance of the moon. Norland found this intriguing, and with his interest in astronomy arrived at a hypothesis that misunderstandings in astronomy, namely cosmological problems are at the core of what lead to this worldwide concoction of so many religions and gods. They all share one common theme. They are a way of explaining our lives in connection with the universe. Upon his return from traveling the world, Norland married, raised a family, built a house, found self employment and continued to research and complete this book, which was inspired from his discoveries in those years of education, search and travel.